Just A Thought
Think on These Things

~

"Finally, brethren, whatever things are true, whatever things are noble, whatever things are just, whatever things are pure, whatever things are lovely, whatever things are of good report, if there is any virtue and if there is anything praiseworthy—meditate on these things."
Philippians 4:8 NKJV

~

By
Danny G. Thomas

FWB
For Worthwhile Books Publications
Columbus, Ohio

Introduction

They say "an idle mind is the Devil's workshop," and I believe that to be true. If you have nothing to think about, Satan will fill your mind with many things to think about. If you love God and think about Him, your mind will quickly go to the many blessings that He sends your way; Your mind will be fixed upon Him.

We read in **Philippians 4:8:** *"Finally, brethren, whatever things are true, whatever things are noble, whatever things are just, whatever things are pure, whatever things are lovely, whatever things are of good report, if there is any virtue and if there is anything praiseworthy—meditate on these things."* **NKJV**

This is a no-brainer, isn't it? Certainly, truthful things, noble things, pure things, lovely things and things that are of good intent have virtue and the element of praise within them. It is certain that all who meditate on such things are much the better for it.

My aim is to bring some of these things to the forefront of your mind and encourage you to think about them for a moment. I believe we will see together that life is so much the better for these moments together.

Danny G. Thomas

Dedication

To our children, grandchildren, great-grandchildren,
future family, and all who come behind us.

A Servant's Prayer

Dear Heavenly Father,
Because I am Your child, I am blessed.

You have loved me eternally,
Cared for me faithfully,
And saved me through the gift of Your Son Jesus.

Just as You have lifted me up, Lord,
Let me also lift up others in a spirit of encouragement,
Optimism, and hope.

Today, and every day, let me share the healing message
of Your son,
And let me leave this world a little better than I found it,
Whether through a genuine smile,
A firm handshake,
A kind word,
Or a heartfelt prayer.
Unknown

Found in my Dad, Glenn E. Thomas' notes.
From the book: ***Promises and Prayers for a Woman's Heart***

"Today is mine; tomorrow is none of my business. If I peer anxiously into the fog of the future, I will strain my spiritual eyes so that I will not see clearly what is required of me now." **Elizabeth Elliott**

"My little children, I am writing these things to you so that you may not sin. But if anyone does sin, we have an advocate with the father, Jesus Christ the righteous."
1 John 2:1 ESV

*- **Poppy and Grammy***

Information About the Author

Reverend Danny G. Thomas has ministered in the areas of youth and music, Christian education, and in pastoral care for more than 44 years. He is a writer and is the author of several devotional books. He is a speaker, teacher, encourager, and student of the Bible.

Danny and his wife Barbara (Bobbie) live in Albany, Georgia. They have made several trips to Sapporo and Tokyo, Japan where they have worked in various ministries with their daughter and son-in-law, Joni and Heath Hubbard. They have also taken a group of high school juniors and seniors to Tokyo for a short-term mission work in 2016. Danny has been to China and North Korea with the "Sons of Jubal," a Men's Chorus that is comprised of over 250 Ministers of Music and Pastors and is a ministry of the Georgia Baptist Convention.

Danny and his wife are presently members of Sherwood Baptist Church in Albany, Georgia, where they are actively involved in the Worship Ministry. His heart is to encourage the believer, challenge the unbeliever, and make the Word of God clear, applicable, and a very present help to people in their lives today by helping them to think about God's Word and to apply God's Word.

Table of Contents

Day 1:
Armed with The Mind of Christ
Philippians 4:1

"Since therefore Christ suffered in the flesh, arm yourselves with the same way of thinking, for whoever has suffered in the flesh has ceased from sin." **1 Peter 4:1 ESV**

How you think is how you live. How you live displays how you think. Who or what you treasure and who or what you love consumes your thinking, your time, and it defines why you do what you do. You glory in what you think and give honor to those thoughts all throughout the day.

Jesus came to do the will of the Father. He loved the Father, and all that He did was to give glory the Father. He lived for the Father, suffered for the Father, fulfilled the will of the Father, and died for the Father. The mind of Christ was toward the Father, and He desired that those who followed Him would do as He did.

This is the example for us who follow Jesus. We will have to suffer for Jesus, and some more than others, but all believers will suffer for their following Jesus. How we do battle is to have the same mind that Jesus had. We are given grace to endure and mercy when we fail. Suffering today for the cause of Christ will make it easier to suffer for the cause of Christ tomorrow. It is a joy to follow Christ because He gives us joy and more joy. He gives us peace, and we feel contented in those times. Why? It is because the peace of God is not like the peace of this

11

world. It is a peace of mind. For this time we have on earth is temporary, and eternity is ours.

"Since therefore Christ suffered in the flesh, arm yourselves with the same way of thinking, for whoever has suffered in the flesh has ceased from sin." **1 Peter 4:1 ESV**

Think about it. *Selah*

Day 2:
Trust and Obey

"Trust in the Lord with all your heart, and do not lean on your own understanding." **Proverbs 3:5-6 ESV**

As I was growing up, a hymn that was sung so often was "Trust and Obey." Do you know that song? Have you sung those lyrics? The lyrics of "Trust and Obey" were written in 1887 by Rev. John H. Sammis, a Presbyterian minister who taught at the Bible Institute of Los Angeles. During an after-service testimony meeting at one of Dwight L. Moody's revival meetings, a young man stood up and concluded his testimony by saying, "I'm not quite sure, but I'm going to trust, and I'm going to obey." Daniel Towner, who was a composer and music director at Moody Bible Institute in Chicago, Illinois, wrote down those few words and sent them to Rev. Sammis, who then developed those words into the song "Trust and Obey."

Notice the first verse and chorus of this song:

When we walk with the Lord in the light of His Word,
What a glory He sheds on our way.
While we do His good will, He abides with us still,
And with all who will trust and obey.

Trust and obey, for there is no other way
To be happy in Jesus,
But to trust and obey.

If you want to live a happy life and an overcoming life, it is necessary for you to trust God. Having our trust in Him and understanding His Word to us, we <u>MUST</u> then obey what we know and hear. Obedience is the confirmation of what we know. Doing what you know to do brings about happiness.

Notice the key things in these lyrics:

1. Walk with God daily.
2. Read the Word for a light in your walk.
3. Listen for God's voice throughout the day.
4. Obey what you hear God tell you in the walk.
5. God will be with you as you obey His word.
6. Trusting God and obeying God is the only way to be happy in life.

It is not necessary to understand God but it is necessary to trust God and obey God.

"For at one time you were darkness, but now you are light in the Lord. Walk as children of light." **Ephesians 5:8 ESV**

Think about it. *Selah*

Day 3:
Are You Frustrated?

"Be angry, and do not sin; ponder in your own hearts on your beds, and be silent. Selah." **Psalm 4:4 ESV**

Is there something in your life that you cannot understand and it brings up anger and confusion? Is it God that you are wondering about? Are you asking yourself, why? Is there something that you can do to solve this state of confusion, anxiety, and yes, anger?

May I remind you that it was Job who, by the description of God's own words, was the most righteous man on the earth at his time and who vented great anger at God for what was happening to him. He could not see any justification for what had happened. He knew in his heart that he strived with all his being to be obedient to God, and his friends knew it as well. So why?

The problem was that Job did not see that God allowed all of the terrible and unfair things to happen to him to make a point to Satan. I think that Job never found out the answer until his earthly life came to an end and he stood before God.

The same is true for us. There will be many bad and unfair things that will happen in our lives just because we live in a bad and unfair world that is controlled by Satan. Yet, in spite of these things, God will satisfy us if we will be still and listen.

David in **Psalm 4:1** expresses such a time of confusion: *"Answer me when I call, O God of my* *righteousness! You have given me relief when I was in distress. Be gracious to me and hear my prayer!"* **ESV**

In **vs. 4** David gives an answer and solution to us: *"Be angry, and do not sin; ponder in your own hearts on your beds, and be silent."* **ESV**

This is a solution that I would like to recommend to you: Find a place somewhere that you can be alone and unhindered. Leave any phone or other communication device that would interrupt you and get alone with God. Then vent all the frustration and points of anger that are attacking you right now. Vent them all before God with all the emotion that is connected with them, and then sit back or lie down and be quiet. Be still. Stay there for an hour or two or a day or two just being quiet. Soon, there will be a still small voice that you will hear as you feel the great arms of God envelope you. His great love will overcome you, and He will speak to you. He will answer your questions and objections, and you will experience that peace that passes all understanding. Just be quiet and be still.

In **Psalm 46:10 ESV** we read: *"Be still and <u>know</u> that I am God."* Yes, if you will just be still for a while you will come to find out that it is God who holds all things together by His mighty hand and that same hand keeps us together. God loves His sheep and cares for them. You can know the answers to your questions but first you must be still.

"Be angry, and do not sin; ponder in your own hearts on your beds, and be silent. Selah." **Psalm 4:4 ESV**

Think about it. *Selah!*

Day 4:
What If I Could Give You a Guarantee?

"Who shall bring any charge against God's elect? It is God who justifies. Who is to condemn? Christ Jesus is the one who died—more than that, who was raised—who is at the right hand of God, who indeed is interceding for us."
Romans 8:33-34 ESV

If you were to die today, are you certain that you would go to heaven? What if I could give you a guarantee that you can know for certain, would that help you?

Do you believe that there is only one God? If so, do you believe that the Bible is the Word of God? If you do, do you believe that God is the Creator of the heavens and the earth? Then do you believe that Satan is the author of sin and it was he who tricked Adam and Eve to disobey God in the garden where God created them? Do you understand because of this act, mankind is now born a sinner and apart from God? If that is your belief, do you believe that now all mankind is helplessly lost and apart from God with no way of closing that gap of separation and doomed to spend eternity in hell?

Having said all of that, let me further press my questioning. Do you believe that the only reason that God the Father sent Jesus was to pay the price for the sins of the whole world for everyone who would believe that?

If your answers have been yes to the preceding questioning, let me ask one more question. Who is it that said what was written in **John 3:16**? It was Jesus Himself. Now let me tell you that God cannot lie, and if Jesus is God's only begotten Son and He said this, it must be guaranteed as true based upon His faithfulness.

We read in **Romans 8:33-34 ESV,** *"Who shall bring any charge against God's elect? It is God who justifies. Who is to condemn? Christ Jesus is the one who died— more than that, who was raised—who is at the right hand of God, who indeed is interceding for us."*

If you realize that you are hopelessly lost, the only solution then, is to find a hope outside of you. Jesus is Hope itself, and God the Father sent His Son Jesus as the solution for sin; He sent Him to die for the penalty of sin and thereby to justify His desire to have you in His presence for eternity. This being true by the very Word of God, then, who is it in heaven or earth that could justifiably object? The answer is no one.

If there is no legitimate objection for God welcoming you into His heaven, the offer is guaranteed. Notice what John writes in **1 John 5:13,** *"I write these things to you who believe in the name of the Son of God, that you may know that you have eternal life. And this is the confidence that we have toward him, that if we ask anything according to his will he hears us."* **ESV**

Did you know that God does not want you to be unsure of your place in His sight? He wants you to be confident and certain; therefore, He gives you His solemn Word. He gives greater insight in **2 Corinthians 5:21 ESV,** *"For our sake he made him to be sin that knew no sin, so that in him we might become the righteousness of God."* This means that you have been made new. It means that you are no longer a sin-stained creation but a new creation. All the old things of your life have been done away with and you are brand new. The **New Living Translation** uses these words: *"For God made Christ, who never sinned, to be the offering for our sin, so that we could be made right with God through Christ."* Don't you just love that? That is our guarantee. *"He who has prepared us for this very thing is God, who has given us the Spirit as a guarantee."* **2 Corinthians 5:5 ESV**

The work for our eternal life has been done for you by God. It is all His idea. It is all His work and there is nothing else that needs to be done because *"He has done all things well,"* **Mark 7:37 ESV.** The only thing we can do is to **accept His great gift**. *"Whoever believes in him is not condemned, but whoever does not believe is condemned already, because he has not believed in the name of the only Son of God."* **John 3:18 ESV**

This is a sure thing and a guaranteed thing. You can trust in God's Word and His special and only plan. If there were another way, then Jesus would not have come.

Think about it. *Selah!*

Day 5:
Be Prepared

"But I will stay in Ephesus until Pentecost, for a wide door for effective work has opened to me, and there are many adversaries. **1 Corinthians 16:8-9 ESV**

"Be Prepared!" This is the motto of the Boy Scouts. Being prepared for what one might confront can make the difference in success or failure. Being prepared for the future is why we send our children to college or trade school. We want our children to have the needed knowledge to make decisions with confidence and move with assurance.

It's like the story of two boys running from a bear, and one stops and puts on his tennis shoes. The other boy says, "Why are you wasting time putting on tennis shoes? Don't you understand that there is a bear chasing us?" The boy then responds to his friend, "I don't have to outrun the bear. I just have to outrun you." The first boy was prepared for the situation, and the other was not.

The bear was bad news but the tennis shoes were the preparation. We need to be prepared to take advantage of good opportunities that may present themselves to us as well. Opportunities can be described as "open doors" in our lives. When a door opens we must be prepared to go through that door. If we are not prepared to take advantage of the opportunity, the door will close and the one that is prepared will benefit.

So what am I saying? I'm saying be prepared for open doors but do not look for open doors where you are not prepared. Paul was prepared and recognized the *"wide door"* that was opened for *"effective work."* There may have been other things that he could have done but the *"wide door"* that was before him was the right door.

Studying prepares the individual. Training prepares the person. Gaining abilities, knowledge, and understanding prepares one for good things ahead and the bad things as well. Being prepared also helps prepare others. It is to your benefit and the benefit of others to go through the right open door. Remember, the wrong open door is a temptation; the right open door is a blessing.

We read in **Ephesians 6:13 – 20** about being prepared. One of the preparations or "readiness" is putting on the whole armor of God that we might be able to withstand the schemes of the devil. We need to be ready for scheming deeds. We are also to pray about all things and at all times that we might be able to "persevere" in life. We need the support of fellow believers who are prepared as well.

So, be prepared. Be prepared for opportunities where God might use you and be prepared where Satan will oppose you. In all of these preparations God remains faithful. We can be sure that He who began a good work in us will be faithful to the end. We only need to be prepared, to be observant, and to be obedient. Look for open doors and be on the alert or prepared for the schemes of the devil.

"But I will stay in Ephesus until Pentecost, for a wide door for effective work has opened to me, and there are many adversaries. **1 Corinthians 16:8-9 ESV**

Think about it. *Selah!*

Day 6:
Why Did I Say That?

"For he did not know what to say, for they were terrified." **Mark 9:6 ESV**

Peter, James, and John were with Jesus on a mountain when all of a sudden they saw before them Jesus transfigured in the clouds with Moses and Elijah. They were terrified by the situation, and everyone was speechless but Peter. Peter relates this event to Mark and Mark records it in **Mark 9:6**. Peter acknowledges that he and the other two were frightened and he speaks, *"Rabbi, it is good that we are here. Let us make three tents, one for you and one for Moses and one for Elijah."* **Mark 9:5 ESV**

It seemed like a good thing, but the glory of Jesus was not to be shared with anyone. He alone must receive the glory. The voice of the Father spoke up to say, *"This is my beloved Son; listen to him,"* **Mark 9:7 ESV**. Moses and Elijah spoke of Jesus and only Jesus was left to be glorified there after it was over.

I have been in situations where the conversation dropped and no one was saying anything. I thought that I needed to say something and spoke up with some careless words, but what I said made no sense, was misunderstood or at least confusing. As soon as I finished I thought, "Why didn't I just keep silent?"

The truth is *silence is golden* and time does not have to be filled with meaningless words. Silence makes people think. If you don't know what to say, don't say anything.

Have you ever been in a situation where you told someone something, and afterwards you wished you had said nothing? I'm sure you have. I'm sure you have said something in jest or flippantly without thinking, and someone was offended. Your action had embarrassed you. You probably thought to yourself, "I should have just been quiet."

The old adage is true: *"Silence is Golden."* Mark Twain has been credited with the statement, *"It is better to be thought to be a fool, than to open your mouth and remove all doubt."* We read in **Proverbs 17:28 ESV**, *"Even a fool who keeps silent is considered wise"* and in **Ecclesiastes 10:14 ESV**, *"A fool multiplies words."*

It is best to think before you speak and to consider the situation. Paul writes in
1 Thessalonians 5:17 ESV to *"pray without ceasing"* and in **1 Timothy 2:8 ESV**, *"I desire then that in every place the men should pray, lifting holy hands without anger or quarreling."*

So, if you do not want to embarrass yourself or unintentionally offend someone, be a person of few words and well-placed words. If you don't know what to say, don't say anything. Think about what you say and remember Peter.

"For he did not know what to say, for they were terrified."
Mark 9:6

Think about it. *Selah!*

Day 7:
Transformed

"For those whom he foreknew he also predestined to be conformed to the image of his Son, in order that he might be the firstborn among many brothers. And those whom he predestined he also called, and those whom he called he also justified, and those whom he justified he also glorified." **Romans 8:29-30 ESV**

God knows you. God knows you so well that He knows all that you will ever have a need of before you even think about the fact that you need it, **Matthew 6:8.** Before the first act of creation was commanded, God already knew you, **Psalm 139:16.**

God doesn't learn of your needs; He knows of your needs. Do you realize that all your needs God *will* supply and not just supply but He will supply them abundantly? Now, we are not God, but we are His children. He loves His children, but when they ask for things that might harm them, He will not give those things because it is His great desire to conform them to His image.

God does not want His children to be unlike Him but to be "like" Him. His gifts conform us into His likeness.

This is what I what you to understand: A growing child of God will experience difficulties and trying times in order that he might be conformed into a likeness of God. You see, God knows what we have need of before we ask or before we understand that we have that need. Sometimes what we think we need is not really what we actually need. We really don't see things as they actually are but God does, and He is actively working all things together for our good to transform us into glorious children of God.

If we answer the call of God, He justifies us and glorifies us by conforming us into the very image of His Son Jesus. We are covered with His righteousness and made a new creation by that work of conformation, **2 Corinthians 5:21, Ephesians 2:4-10.**

Have you been praying about something? Don't worry. God hears your prayer but He has already made provisions to meet the real need that you have. Trust Him, be patient, and be thankful that God knows.

"For those whom he foreknew he also predestined to be conformed to the image of his Son, in order that he might be the firstborn among many brothers. And those he predestined he also called, and those whom he called he also justified, and those whom he justified he also glorified." **Romans 8:29-30 ESV**

Think about it. *Selah!*

Day 8:
Get Your Act Together

"But God, being rich in mercy, because of the great love with which he loved us, even when we were dead in our trespasses, made us alive together with Christ—by grace you have been saved—and raised us up with him and seated us with him in the heavenly places in Christ Jesus."
Ephesians 2:4-5 ESV

God didn't tell us to get our act together. His act made it possible for us to be brought together with Him in heaven. You see, we cannot get our act together. We must be made anew, and that is exactly what God did for us through His Son Jesus.

God wants you, as you are, to make you what you cannot be. It is impossible to get your act together, and it is impossible to be ready for heaven or ready to be saved other than to admit that you are totally helpless on your own. The good news is that God is totally ready and willing to make you into that new creation if you will obey and answer His call to you.

It's like the old invitation song we used to sing that was used by the evangelist Billy Graham in his services, "Just As I Am." The lyrics are, *"Just as I am without one plea, but that Thy blood was shed for me."* What is our plea? It is guilty and you must throw yourself at the mercy of the court. Jesus takes that helpless plea and pours His blood upon it. He pours His righteous, pure, and holy blood upon our guilty and helpless soul, and thereby we are made righteous, pure, and holy. Jesus shed His blood for us because of our sin and because He loves us and desires for us to spend eternity with Him in His heaven.

Are you still trying to get your life straight? That will never happen. Jesus is holding His hand out for you with His gift of a pure life and wants to make you into a new creation.

Jesus has it all together so come just as you are, and He will make you into what you cannot be.

"But God, being rich in mercy, because of the great love with which he loved us, even when we were dead in our trespasses, made us alive together with Christ—by grace you have been saved—and raised us up with him and seated us with him in the heavenly places in Christ Jesus." **Ephesians 2:4-5 ESV**

Think about it. *Selah!*

Day 9:
You Don't Have to Understand

"Who is this that hides counsel without knowledge? Therefore I have uttered what I did not understand, things too wonderful for me, which I did not know." **Job 42:3 ESV**

When my younger son Jeremy was five years old, we discovered that he had a narrowing in his esophagus that would sometimes cause food to become unable to pass through. Three times we found ourselves in the emergency room having the food dislodged. It was a very frightening time. Our pediatrician recommended that we take Jeremy to have surgery on his esophagus at Egleston Children's Hospital at Emory in Atlanta. We took his advice and made arrangements.

As the time approached for the operation to take place, we were placed in a wing of the hospital that cared for children with that same special problem. A team of doctors and medical students were going through the wing discussing the various cases with each other. My wife was listening and mentioned to one of the doctors, "I really don't understand how this procedure works." The doctor looked at her and said, "You don't need to understand. You're not a doctor."

This is how we often are with God. We approach God and say, "Why don't you do this, or I just don't understand how this is going to turn out?" The truth is we don't need to understand; we just need to obey and follow His commands to us. God has everything under control. For with God all things are possible and there is nothing too hard for God.

I love the old Ira Stanphill song, "I Know Who Holds Tomorrow." The lyrics of the first verse and chorus are:

I don't know about tomorrow,
I just live from day to day;
I don't borrow from its sunshine,
For its skies may turn to gray;

I don't worry o'er the future,
For I know what Jesus said;
And today I'll walk beside Him,
For He knows what is ahead.

Many things about tomorrow,
I don't seem to understand;
But I know who holds tomorrow,
And I know who holds my hand.

We don't need to know all things; we only need to know Him Who knows all things. We also need to be in His hand.

"Who is this that hides counsel without knowledge? Therefore I have uttered what I did not understand, things too wonderful for me, which I did not know." **Job 42:3 ESV**

Think about it. *Selah!*

Day 10:
You Ask a Hard Thing

"When they had crossed, Elijah said to Elisha, 'Ask what I shall do for you, before I am taken from you.' And Elisha said, 'Please let there be a double portion of your spirit on me.' And he said, 'You have asked a hard thing; yet, if you see me as I am being taken from you, it shall be so for you, but if you do not see me, it shall not be so.' "
2 Kings 2:9-10 ESV

Elijah was a mighty man of God and his protégé, Elisha, stood in awe of him admiring the mighty things that God had done through him. This student wanted not only to be as mighty as Elijah but also to have twice as much of the power of God upon him as Elijah did.

Actually that was not something that Elijah could provide, it was something that only God was able to provide because it came from God, not from Elijah. The power of God was upon Elijah, and it was God who did those things. Elijah was expressing this to Elisha. Elijah was saying that if God allows you to see me being taken away from you by a mighty act of God, then God would provide what you are asking for.

Elisha did see Elijah taken up into heaven and God did give a double portion of the Holy Spirit upon Elisha. We read many times in Scripture where hard, difficult, and even impossible things were asked of God and Jesus that were granted and accomplished. The angel said to Mary, *"For nothing will be impossible with God,"* **Luke 1:37 ESV**. To the father who asked of Jesus, if you can would you free my son of a demon, *"And Jesus said to him, 'If you can!'*

*All things are possible for one who believes," **Mark 9:23 ESV.*** The response of the father was a reflection of our faith most times, *"I believe; help my unbelief,"* **Vs. 24.**

Is there a hard thing in your life that you are dealing with? Do you feel that it might be too burdensome to ask of God? Perhaps this hard thing is a besetting sin in your life and you have knelt before God more times than you want to admit. Perhaps you feel God may be tired of hearing the same thing again. The answer is *"If I can!"* Your attitude is humorous to Jesus because it is not whether He is listening, the question is, "Are you believing?" Of course, He can help you, and of course He is not tired of listening to His child.

No, this is not a hard thing for God; it is a hard thing for you. You will conquer this hard thing in your life if you watch for the hand of God. If you will draw near to God and listen to His voice (through Scripture, the still small voice in your life) your request will be granted.

Man cannot solve the problem because it is not for him to solve, but it can be solved with God. In the meantime, keep on believing and seek God's help in your unbelief. When you see God, when your eyes are fixed on Him, this hard thing will be taken from you.

Here are four things to consider:

1. Ask
2. Trust
3. Look
4. Believe

"And he said, 'You have asked a hard thing; yet, if you see me as I am being taken from you, it shall be so for you, but if you do not see me, it shall not be so.'"
2 Kings 2:10 ESV

Think about it. *Selah!*

Day 11:
Just Leave It There

"Come to me, all who labor and are heavy laden, and I will give you rest. Take my yoke upon you, and learn from me, for I am gentle and lowly in heart, and you will find rest for your souls. For my yoke is easy, and my burden is light."
Matthew 11:28-30 ESV

Leave it there and forget it. Too often we want to revisit, remind, and remain there. Things that bother us do so because we are continually taking them up, rethinking them, and reliving them over again.

There are things in our lives that need to be rethought and relived so that we can learn from them. That is part of the learning process of life. Investing in our resources will benefit us and help us to learn, but when we have been given a solution to a problem or a cure for a problem, we should not continually handle those thorns and revisit those infestations.

The heavy things in our lives are those things that drain us, strain us, and deplete our energy and take away the joy and happiness in life. Jesus tells us to take our burdens, those heavy things in life, to Him. He wants to share His yoke with us. The yoke does not take the burden and heavy thing away; it makes it easy and light. Jesus shares in our lives and makes life restful and pleasant.

Remember Jesus told us that we are to expect trouble in this world. We are to understand that there will be times of heaviness and extreme times of testing. Then He adds, "I have overcome the world," **John 16:33 ESV.** He is with us, for us, and in us. We can depend upon that.

So, those things that are causing you to strain can be made easy if you will take them to Jesus and leave them with Him. Don't take them up again. Just leave them there and life will remain easy and light with Him. Don't question and don't rethink and evaluate matters. Just stay under His yoke and walk beside Him.

The chorus of the old hymn "Leave It There" written by Charles A. Tindley says,

> *Leave it there, leave it there,*
> *Take your burden to the Lord and leave it there;*
> *If you trust and never doubt,*
> *He will surely bring you out;*
> *Take your burden to the Lord and leave it there.*

Life on earth is troublesome and difficult, but we don't have to go through life alone. We have a Savior and a load sharer, and that is Jesus Christ who will never leave us or forsake us. Jesus is always with us and wants to help in our times of heaviness.

> *If the world from you withhold of its silver and its gold,*
> *And you have to get along with meager fare,*
> *Just remember, in His Word how He feeds the little bird;*
> *Take your burden to the Lord and leave it there.*

> *Leave it there, leave it there,*
> *Take your burden to the Lord and leave it there;*
> *If you trust and never doubt,*
> *He will surely bring you out;*

Take your burden to the Lord and leave it there.
Charles A. Tendley

"Come to me, all who labor and are heavy laden, and I will give you rest. Take my yoke upon you, and learn from me, for I am gentle and lowly in heart, and you will find rest for your souls. For my yoke is easy, and my burden is light."
Matthew 11:28-30 ESV

If Jesus has it, forget it and leave it with Him!

Think about it. *Selah!*

Day 12:
Please Excuse Me for A Moment

"And if I go and prepare a place for you, I will come again and will take you to myself, that where I am you may be also." **John 14:3 ESV**

Death is a difficult subject for most of us, but it doesn't have to be. Death is a door, a passageway to another room. Remember when Jesus said that in His Father's house, there are many "rooms." **John 14:2 ESV**

Henry Scott Holland (1847 – 1918), Regius Professor of Divinity at the University of Oxford, the canon of Christ Church, Oxford, and priest at St. Paul's Cathedral of London, wrote the following on death as part of a sermon in 1910. I have found it useful in the lives of many at the time of death.

"Death is nothing at all. It does not count. I have only slipped away into the next room. Nothing has happened. Everything remains exactly as it was. I am I, and you are you, and the old life that we lived so fondly together is untouched, unchanged. Whatever we were to each other, that we are still. Call me by the old familiar name. Speak of me in the easy way which you always used. Put no difference into your tone. Wear no forced air of solemnity or sorrow. Laugh as we always laughed at the little jokes that we enjoyed together. Play, smile, think of me, pray for me. Let my name be ever the household word that it always was. Let it be spoken without an effort, without the ghost of a shadow upon it. Life means all that it ever meant. It is the same as it ever was. There is absolute and unbroken continuity. What is this death but a negligible

accident? Why should I be out of mind because I am out of sight? I am but waiting for you, for an interval, somewhere very near, just round the corner. All is well." **Henry Scott Holland**

Dr. Holland has described death well. Yes, this life is but a moment, but life eternal is with Christ Jesus forever. It is this life that we are preparing for eternity. Our eternity will be spent either in unending life or eternal and unending death. It is only when eternity has not been prepared for should there be any question, fear, or cause for concern. Unending death is eternal separation.

For the believer our eternity is in the hands of God. Though we may not completely understand things now, as we step into the other room we will have full understanding and see the full picture. *"For now we see in a mirror dimly, but then face to face. Now I know in part; then I shall know fully, even as I have been fully known."* **1 Corinthians 13:12**

"And if I go and prepare a place for you, I will come again and will take you to myself, that where I am you may be also." **John 14:3 ESV**

Think about it. *Selah!*

Day 13:
Remember?

"Tie them on your finger as a reminder. Write them deep within your heart." **Proverbs 7:3 NLT**

What are some of the remembrances of your past? Are they good, bad, or a mixture? Those memories are some of the events that helped shape you into the person that you are today.

Perhaps your memories are labeled "The Good Ole Days." Or, they may be hurtful pains that you are trying to forget; but they are forever engraved in your mind. They are, nevertheless, the building blocks of your life.

Solomon was reminding his son to remember those lessons, truths, and principles that he had purposefully taught him hoping to make a positive influence on his future. He tells him to tie a *string* around his finger and when he looks at that *string*, the *string* will bring back to his memory those truths that he had been taught by his father.

I want to share with you a letter I wrote to my Mom on her last Mother's Day, 2016, but first I need to give you a little information about my Mom. She lived with my wife and me for 20 years. My Dad lived with us as well, but he died six years earlier. My Mom had Alzheimer's disease, and her mind was captivated by that dreaded disease for at least the last 15 years of her life. It imprisoned her with horrible thoughts and fears that could not be explained to her or reasoned out. We came to the realization that helping her was beyond anything that we were able to do. We were inadequate. Many prayers for her had been placed before the very throne of God. What we perceived as silence from God was not silence at all and was not understood until the last few weeks and months of her life. We worried and wondered, but the *string* reminded us of all that we had been taught through the years. Though she could not speak or encourage us through those times, the *string* of her previous teaching spoke softly and clearly.

God was teaching us many wonderful things and He, as well, tied a *string* around our finger. Although enslaved in the grip of Alzheimer's, my Mom was fully engaged in the ministry in which God had called her until the end of her life. We do not always see how, but God does and He faithfully works daily.

The following is the letter I wrote to my Mom on Mother's Day, 2016:

Mom, when I think of you and when I see you, I remember. To remember is a wonderful thing.

To remember causes one to recall both the good and the bad. To remember will cause a person to repeat in his mind those events of yesterday and creates a learning situation. We learn from the things that we do, and when we repeat them in our minds, we learn. The old adage is *"repetition is the mother of learning"* and it is true.

Solomon writes to his son to treasure the instructions and commandments that he taught him in **Proverbs 7:2**

NLT: *"Tie them on your finger as a reminder. Write them deep within your heart."* So, you are the *string* around my finger, the reminder of the things you and Dad taught us as children. I remember them with deep appreciation and joy. They are fond recounts of my life.

I remember Jesus.
I remember Scripture.
I remember service to God.
I remember dedication, faithfulness, love, care, giving, and receiving.
I remember correction, instruction in righteousness, and your guiding hand.
I remember your soft and loving voice.
I remember laughter, tears of joy, as well as tears of sadness for the tragedy of
    others, but never because of difficulty in our lives.
I remember provision, supply, and needs being met by the mighty hand of God
    just when we needed them the most.

But I do not remember any occasion of doubt, hate, backbiting of others, worry, fret about tomorrow, or straying from the goal of the mission of spreading God's Good News in any way. My only remembrance is of the loyal service to God and to each other.

I remember meeting the needs of others.
I remember having missionaries in our home, preachers in our home, relatives in
    our home, orphans in our home, friends in our home, and strangers in our home.
I remember trips together.
I remember classic events that I will not put in print but are forever engraved in

my mind, in your mind, in Dad's mind, and in each of your children's minds that
   will always bring about laughter.

I remember your beauty all throughout your life.
I remember your mother and dad, brothers and sisters, and the thrill of their
   visits as well as our visits with them.

Yes, I remember all of this and much more, which is all brought about by that *string* around my finger. Mom, you are that *string*. You are that constant reminder, teacher, source of joy, and support.

I want you to remember this Mom: I love you, Bobbie loves you, and each of our children and their children have tied you to their finger, and that *string* brings strength, understanding, joy, and love to them that will never leave them.

That *string* gives us great comfort to feel certain that you have Bobbie and me tied around your finger as well, and that we bring about joy to your remembrance.

Remember, Mom? I do.

"Tie them on your finger as a reminder. Write them deep within your heart." **Proverbs 7:3 NLT**

Think about it. *Selah!*

Day 14:
Push Out into The Deep

"And when he had finished speaking, he said to Simon, 'Put out into the deep and let down your nets for a catch.' " **Luke 5:4 ESV**

Have you ever found yourself in deep water? Most likely you have. To be in deep water is to be in trouble, to find yourself in a situation that you are not prepared for, and one that is difficult and dangerous. You are in a vulnerable and very serious situation that is beyond your ability to handle. Being in deep water is being in a situation where you need the immediate help of someone with greater ability than you.

If you find yourself there, you have been taken by surprise. You didn't mean to be there, or you misread the situation. Perhaps you were overconfident, or the situation changed quickly. If help does not come, you will perish or fall helplessly to a disastrous fate outside of your plans.

There is another scenario, and that is one where someone who is very capable and reliable has taken you into deep waters. In these deep waters, you don't have to be prepared because the One who is taking you knows the deep waters and **is** prepared. In this situation you find rest and enjoyment. This is the same deep water, but it is a pleasant situation that you will remember with great joy the rest of your life. It will prepare you for future situations. To respond to the call of Jesus does not bring about fear to you but rather, enjoyment, and it is profitable to you.

Jesus tells His disciples to push out into the deep water in **Luke 5:4**. He wants to display to them His wisdom and His power, as well as to provide an illustration and an invitation for them to follow Him. Jesus was displaying before them what their mission would be and His ability to be their provider in that mission. They were to follow Him to become fishers of men and to become spreaders of the Good News, the Gospel.

Are you listening? If you hear the voice of Jesus calling you to push out, then push out with Him. Don't worry about your ability because He is your ability. He is your source of strength, and He is your provider and guide. What you must do is only to obey and trust. Respond to His voice and don't consider the water depth. Don't be content with the shallowness at the dock. You can feel confident as you push out into the deep.

Oswald Chambers wrote this is his devotional book, **_My Utmost For His Highest,_** for June 8: *"If you believe in Jesus, you are not to spend all your time in the calm waters just inside the harbor, full of joy, but always tied to the dock. You have to get out past the harbor into the great depths of God, and begin to know things for yourself— begin to have spiritual discernment."* **Oswald Chambers**

So, my challenge to you is to push out or press on. Don't worry about the water depth. Don't look at the troubled waters. Just trust in God. The trio *Selah* sings one of my favorite gospel songs, "Press On."

Ponder these words:

When the valley is deep,
When the mountain is steep,
When the body is weary,
When we stumble and fall.

When the choices are hard,
When we're battered and scarred
When we've spent our resources
When we've given our all.

In Jesus name, we press on!
Dan Burgess

"And when he had finished speaking, he said to Simon, 'Put out into the deep and let down your nets for a catch.' " **Luke 5:4 ESV**

Think about it. *Selah!*

Day 15:
One Thing

"And Jesus, looking at him, loved him, and said to him, 'You lack one thing: go sell all that you have and give it to the poor, and you will have treasure in heaven; and come, follow me.' " Disheartened by the saying, he went away sorrowful, for he had great possessions." **Mark 10:21-22 ESV**

The rich young ruler came to Jesus and posed this question: "What must I do to inherit eternal life?" The response of Jesus to this question was not what he expected. It was that he must sell all that he had and then follow Jesus.

The rich young ruler had everything he could ever desire in this earthly life, and he had acquired all of it either by inheritance or by personal endeavors. He had it all, but there was still one thing he wanted, which was "eternal life." What was the requirement or, perhaps, how much did it cost? Maybe that was in his mind as he asked the question.

Jesus states the obvious thing first, which was that he needed to keep the commandments. This brought about the quick and joyful response of the young ruler that he had kept them "all" from a child. Jesus apparently agreed with him. Jesus loved this young man, and with a loving voice and looking deep into his eyes, He tells him there is only "one thing" in his life that was needed for him to inherit eternal life. That "one thing" was to "sell all" that he had and give all of it to the poor, with the understanding that he would have eternal treasures in heaven which would last throughout eternity. Having done that, he must follow Jesus and eternal life would be his.

The young ruler's reaction was one of sadness and unwillingness to do that "one thing" because he was very rich "now." What he saw on earth was so bright, he could not see the light of eternity. He went away sad and sorrowful.

So, how does this relate to us? Jesus still requires us to "sell all" and to "give" and to follow, but what does that mean? What does it mean to "sell all"?

- Selling all means to give up, to surrender to Jesus.
- Selling all means you can do nothing except through Jesus.
- Selling all means you have nothing but Jesus has everything, and you are totally dependent upon Jesus.
- Selling all means you have no opinion, you have no say-so in ministry and life but to obey the voice of Jesus.
- Selling all means your delight is not in earthly things, but your delight is in Jesus.

Selling all is a personal decision made of your own volition; it's your choice. You cannot join in the battle of **truth** until you have given up the **lies** of life. Jesus asks that you give up "all," the good, bad, and ugly, the best and the worst. He wants you to give it all up. He wants you to follow Him.

Does that make you happy or sad? How will you go away? Consider the lyrics of the song, "I Surrender All":

All to Jesus I surrender,
All to Him I freely give.
I will ever love and trust Him,
In His presence daily live.

I surrender all, I surrender all;
All to Thee, my blessed Savior,
I surrender all.
Judson W. Van DeVenter

"And Jesus, looking at him, loved him, and said to him, 'You lack one thing: go sell all that you have and give it to the poor, and you will have treasure in heaven; and come, follow me.' " Disheartened by the saying, he went away sorrowful, for he had great possessions." **Mark 10:21-22 ESV**

Think about it. *Selah!*

Day 16:
This Needs Salt!

"For everyone will be salted with fire. Salt is good, but if the salt has lost its saltiness, how will you make it salty again? Have salt in yourselves, and be at peace with one another." **Mark 9:49-50 ESV**

Salt is a preservative. Salt is composed primarily of sodium chloride. In its natural form it is a crystal rock substance called rock salt. The ocean has great amounts of salt in it, here are some fresh water bodies of water, such as the Dead Sea in Israel and The Great Salt Lake in the state of Utah, that are so salty it is extremely difficult for a person to sink in it.

Salt was highly prized by the Egyptians, Greeks, and Romans. The Romans would often pay their Legions with salt. Venice fought with Genoa over salt (The Republic of Venetian—The Republic of Genoese Wars 1257 - 1270 & 1294 - 1299). Did you know that *Salad* comes from the practice of the Romans salting vegetable leaves?

In **Mark 9:49-50 ESV**, Jesus tells the people that salt is good but if salt loses its saltiness, then what good is it? He notes that believers must strive to be a preservative or a seasoning to the lives of others. We should make life taste better or last longer by our presence. If we don't, then what good are we to the struggle of earthly life? Jesus proclaimed His message of Heaven and the Kingdom of God, which are eternal, unending. His Kingdom is offered to those who believe.

We are seasoning in life. We add to life, and we ought to make the lives of others more enjoyable. Take a quick look at your life to determine if you are making a seasoned difference, a lasting difference in the lives of others. We are the salt of the earth. We are the salt and light to this world. Have you lost it? Make up your mind today that you will make a difference in the lives of others.

For everyone will be salted with fire. Salt is good, but if the salt has lost its saltiness, how will you make it salty again? Have salt in yourselves, and be at peace with one another." **Mark 9:49-50 ESV**

Think about it. *Selah!*

Day 17:
Hoarded Resources

"As for the rich in this present age, charge them not to be haughty, nor to set their hopes on the uncertainty of riches, but on God, who richly provides us with everything to enjoy. They are to do good, to be rich in good works, to be generous and ready to share, thus storing up treasure for themselves as a good foundation for the future, so that they may take hold of that which is truly life." **1 Timothy 6:17-19 ESV**

A hoarder is a person who has an obsessive-compulsive disorder inclination or pattern of life that is characterized by excessively collecting things and not wanting to get rid of them. Their homes and lands are filled with all types of "things." The collected things are dear to them. Many have a great fear of something that might happen in the future that would come quickly upon them.

My wife says that I don't want to throw anything away, and there may be some truth to that charge. However, since God has blessed me with a wife who will throw away almost anything, together we are just right.

I think all of us worry about the future in some degree and strive to prepare for the unknown in different ways; however, the believer is not to depend upon himself but rather upon God. We don't need to be frivolous and flippant in preparing for the future but to be moderate in all that we do. Anything that is beyond moderate preparation should be turned over to the provision of

God. Our main thing should be to be obedient to God's voice and respond to it.

Ponder the lyrics of this beloved hymn from the pen of Annie Johnson Flint:

He Giveth More Grace

"He giveth more grace when the burdens grow greater;
He sendeth more strength when the labors increase.
To added affliction He addeth His mercy;
To multiplied trials, His multiplied peace.

When we have exhausted our store of endurance,
When our strength has failed ere the day is half done,
When we reach the end of our hoarded resources,
Our Father's full giving is only begun.

His love had no limit; His grace has no measure.
His power has no boundary known unto men.
For out of His infinite riches in Jesus,
He giveth, and giveth, and giveth again!
Annie Johnson Flint

As the apostle Paul writes in **Philippians 4:11 ESV**, *". . . for I have learned in whatever situation I am to be content."* He also wrote, *"Let your reasonableness be known to everyone. The Lord as at hand; do not be anxious about anything, but in everything by prayer and supplication with thanksgiving let your requests be made known to God. And the peace of God, which surpasses all understanding, will guard your hearts and your minds in Christ Jesus."* **Philippians 4:5-7 ESV**

If you are going to hoard anything, hoard trust in God and that will give you an abundant supply of peace, a peace beyond your ability to contain it.

"As for the rich in this present age, charge them not to be haughty, nor to set their hopes on the uncertainty of riches, but on God, who richly provides us with everything to enjoy. They are to do good, to be rich in good works, to be generous and ready to share, thus storing up treasure for themselves as a good foundation for the future, so that they may take hold of that which is truly life." **1 Timothy 6:17-19 ESV**

Think about it. *Selah!*

Day 18:
Don't Go Through Life in Fear When Peace Is An Option

"And the peace of God, which surpasses all understanding, will guard your hearts and your minds in Christ Jesus." **Philippians 4:7 ESV**

There are so many people who have had to hear these words, "The tests are positive. You have Cancer." Those words are devastating. Those words are hard to hear and can create huge degrees of uncertainty in a person's life.

Perhaps you have heard those words or maybe even are experiencing the effect of them right now. For sure you have friends or loved ones who are in its grip at this very moment.

A person needs peace, contentment, understanding and wisdom during this trial.
What is needed is a full understanding of the lasting effects of this trial and why there is fear.

It is a known truth that fear ends where peace begins. Where there is peace, there cannot be fear. Fear and peace cannot co-exist. Did you know that Jesus promises us peace? Did you know that when He ascended to heaven He left the "Comforter" to be with us? Do you remember that He warned His disciples and us that we should expect trouble in the world? If He promised us peace, shouldn't we expect to have it? If we don't have this peace that passes all understanding, **Philippians 4:7**, then we should ask ourselves, why don't we?

If we don't have peace, it is because we believe a lie. That lie is fear of pending death; but this death is not an eternal death, it is an opening or beginning to eternal life. It is the realization of what we have been living for on this temporary earth.

As we live in and on this troubled earth, we must handle things like cancer. Cancer is a fact that is best met head-on, and if we meet it head-on, it will head out. What is Cancer anyway? It is a trial, a difficulty, or a trouble that we might have to deal with, but we should be of good cheer because Jesus has overcome that trial and given us the option of peace. Why fear cancer and the unknown when peace and the known is an option? We should think about the good things listed in **Philippians 4:8-9**.

Think about the lyrics of this hymn written by Caroline V. Sandell-Berg, who has been given the title of "The Fanny Crosby of Sweden":

Day by Day

Day by day and with each passing moment,
Strength I find to meet my trials here.
Trusting in my Father's wise bestowment,
I've no cause for worry or for fear.

He whose heart is kind beyond all measure
Gives unto each day what He deems best,
Lovingly, its part of pain and pleasure,
Mingling toil with peace and rest.
Caroline V. Sandell-Berg

This is the challenge: Why fear anything when peace is an option? It's all up to you. How will you live life? Will you fear or will you trust and experience a peace that passes all our ability to understand?

"And the peace of God, which surpasses all understanding, will guard your hearts and your minds in Christ Jesus." **Philippians 4:7 ESV**

Think about it. *Selah!*

Day 19:
None of Your Business!

"Therefore, do not be anxious about tomorrow, for tomorrow will be anxious for itself. Sufficient for the day is its own trouble." **Matthew 6:34 ESV**

Tomorrow, what will it bring? Are you worried about tomorrow? Too many times we worry ourselves about tomorrow because of problems that came about today. Problems sometimes capture our mind to the point that we can do little today because of our worry about what tomorrow may bring. Often when tomorrow gets here, we come to find out that what we worried about yesterday did not happen as we expected. That problem seemed to work out, or it did not show up at all.

In **Matthew 6,** after having instructed His followers on how to pray, what to pray for, how to live life happily and how to prepare for the future, Jesus tells His followers that they don't need to be worried or live in anxiety about their future needs because the future will have enough trouble as it is. The believer's future is, after all, in God's hands and as He has cared for us in the past, He will do no less today or in the future. We can trust Him and His Son. *"Jesus Christ is the same yesterday and today and forever."* **Hebrew 13:8 ESV**

I like what Elizabeth Elliott has said: *"Today is mine; tomorrow is none of my business. If I peer anxiously into the fog of the future, I will strain my spiritual eyes so that I will not see clearly what is required of me now."* **Elizabeth Elliott**

Don't worry about tomorrow because it is in God's hands. Our hope is in Him and *"hope does not disappoint,"* **Romans 5:5 NKJV;** therefore, it is *"none of our business."* Take care of today, this very moment, and leave the rest to God. We have things to do right now, so we should do them. Our future is in Christ and it is sure. Leave it with Him.

What is it that is worrying you? Don't worry; just take care of what you need to do right now. Worry only causes you harm, **Psalm 37:8 NKJV.**

Below is a prayer I found in some of my Dad's notes. I believe it was taken from a book my Mom had entitled, *Promises and Prayers for a Woman's Heart.* The writer is unknown to me. Pray this prayer, put it into action, and then rest in your Heavenly Father.

Dear Heavenly Father,
Because I am Your child, I am blessed.

You have loved me eternally,
Cared for me faithfully,
And saved me through the gift of Your Son Jesus.

Just as You have lifted me up, Lord,
Let me also lift up others in a spirit of encouragement,
Optimism, and hope.

Today, and every day, let me share the healing message of Your son,
And let me leave this world a little better than I found it,
Whether through a genuine smile,
A firm handshake,
A kind word,

Or a heartfelt prayer.
Unknown

Care for the people in your life and the people that you meet. Pray with them, care for them, and encourage them, and you will forget about tomorrow. After all, *"It's none of your business."*

"Therefore, do not be anxious about tomorrow, for tomorrow will be anxious for itself. Sufficient for the day is its own trouble." **Matthew 6:34 ESV**

Think about it. *Selah!*

Day 20:
Never B♭, Never B#, But Always
B♮

"Only let each person lead the life that the Lord has assigned to him, and to which God has called him. This is my rule in all the churches. **1 Corinthians 7:17 ESV**

I was given a framed needlepoint to place on my bookshelf with the writing, "Never B♭, Never B#, But Always B♮" (natural). I think we all might live a much happier life if we had that attitude.

Being natural means to be as you are. Did you know that this is the only way you can come to God? In order to become a Christian, you must come as you are. God expects nothing less and nothing more. You see, He knows you as you are, and He knows you better than you know yourself.

The old invitation song *"Just as I Am,"* written by Charlotte Elliott, states this truth well:

> *Just as I am, without one plea,*
> *But that Thy blood was shed for me,*
> *And that Thou bidd'st me come to Thee*
>   *O Lamb of God, I come, I come.*

> *Just as I am, Thou wilt receive,*
> *Wilt welcome, pardon, cleanse, relieve,*
> *Because Thy promise I believe,*
> *O Lamb of God, I come, I come.*
> **Charlotte Elliot**

Did you get that? *"Without one plea."* There is no excuse you can offer. There is nothing you can do except come as you are, as God sees you. There is nothing that you must do first. You cannot get your life together or get things right or straight. You can only come as you are. And you must come now because today is the appointed time for you. Your only plea is the blood of Jesus that was shed especially for you, for this day, and for this time.

There is only the bidding, which is the still small voice of Jesus, the Lamb of God saying come. If you have not done that, then now is the time. He has promised that He will forgive you and make you a new creation. Old things will be gone, all things of the past, and all things will be made new, **2 Corinthians 5:17-19 & 21.**

Just be natural, or be yourself, and come just as you are. Jesus will make you into what you cannot be without Him. You will become a new creation with a new purpose and will be given a new assignment designed just for you.

"Only let each person lead the life that the Lord has assigned to him, and to which God has called him. This is my rule in all the churches. **1 Corinthians 7:17 ESV**

Think about it. *Selah!*

Day 21:
Stupid

"Whoever loves discipline loves knowledge, but he who hates reproof is stupid." **Proverbs 12:1 ESV**

David writes in **Psalm 92:6,** *"The stupid man cannot know; the fool cannot understand this: that though the wicked sprout like grass and all evildoers flourish, they are doomed to destruction forever;"* **ESV**

In the movie *Forrest Gump,* the lead character, Forrest, says: "Momma always told me: Stupid is as stupid does." No one wants to be called stupid or be thought to be a stupid person. *The New World Dictionary* defines stupid as: "Lack of normal intelligence or understanding, slow witted, dull; the incapacity to perceive, to learn." Solomon says that a stupid person is one that hates reproof or correction. David writes that a stupid man cannot know, cannot understand, and is doomed for destruction forever. There is no help for a stupid person.

Have you ever made a stupid choice or decision? I am sure you have, but this does not mean that you are beyond help. If you recognize that choice or action as stupid, it means that you are not stupid because a stupid person cannot learn and does not recognize wrong as wrong.

Many times, we find ourselves just a step away from stupid but, all of a sudden, a correction is made in our path, and we are saved from that stupid action. This is the Holy Spirit in our lives saying, "No, that is not the way." At that time it is up to us to listen or fall and have to learn from our stupid move.

So, learn to appreciate discipline, benefit from reproof, and respond to the guiding voice of God. Live your life by learning from life, learning God's Word, and patterning your life according to God's Word. In order to be the man or woman that God would have you to be, seek to live by faith and in His will.

One more thing, there is a fine line between bravery and stupidity. Bravery is obeying God and doing what He has called you to do. Bravery is doing God's will for you despite the opposition. Stupidity, on the other hand, is doing your own thing and what feels right to you regardless of the warning from God and opposition.

Psalm 92:6: *"The stupid man cannot know; the fool cannot understand this: that though the wicked sprout like grass and all evildoers flourish, they are doomed to destruction forever;"* **ESV**

"Whoever loves discipline loves knowledge, but he who hates reproof is stupid." **Proverbs 12:1 ESV**

Think about it. *Selah!*

Day 22:
Putting Away Childish Things

"When I was a child, I spoke like a child, I thought like a child, I reasoned like a child. When I became a man, I gave up childish ways. For now we see in a mirror dimly, but then face to face. Now I know in part; then I shall know fully, even as I have been fully known." **1 Corinthians 13:11-12 ESV**

"Don't act like a baby!" Have you ever been told that? I'm sure you have, and I am also sure that if you raised children, you have said that to one or all of your children many times, if not multiple times.

In the life of believers, we too have come to the realization that our actions were childish. Why was it that we acted as we did? Perhaps if we were to take an honest look at the situation, we would come to the conclusion that we were selfish in our perception or that we misread the situation.

I will have to admit that I have been in those situations many times. I misread things so easily. I assume that an action is concocted with the intentions that I ascribe to it and get angry and act like a child rather than a man that I am. I look through the glass dimly. I look into the mirror, but the mirror is curved, stained, or contorted so that I cannot see clearly.

What needs to be done is to look through the eyes of God, not the mirror of my making or of someone else's. To look through the eyes of God is to see clearly. To look through the eyes of God is to see the actual thing and not an image.   Through God's eyes we see needs and opportunity to minister and represent Him. We have put away the childish, selfish, and self-beneficial reasoning and ways. This ministry I have been called to do is about two things: It's all about Him and them. I am to go to them for Him.

So, I am now going to make a promise to myself that I will quit acting like a child and will make a grand effort to see things through the eyes of God as a mature believer in Christ Jesus.

What about you? Have you put away childish things?

"When I was a child, I spoke like a child, I thought like a child, I reasoned like a child. When I became a man, I gave up childish ways. For now we see in a mirror dimly, but then face to face. Now I know in part; then I shall know fully, even as I have been fully known." **1 Corinthians 13:11-12 ESV**

Think about it. *Selah!*

Day 23:
Fleeing Youthful Passions

"So flee youthful passions and pursue righteousness, faith, love, and peace, along with those who call on the Lord from a pure heart. **2 Timothy 2:22 ESV**

A pure and holy passion! Passion is not bad but when passion is focused upon that which is not holy, good, and right, it is misguided and is sin.

In **2 Timothy 2:22,** the Apostle Paul tells his protégé, Timothy, to run from the passions in his life that are driven by his youthful desires. A desire that is not God's desire is a wrong desire. Did you know that God wants only that which is best for us? **Jeremiah 29:11:** *"For I know the plans I have for you, declares the Lord, plans for welfare and not for evil, to give you a future and a hope."* **ESV**

A great caution in life is that youthful passions often do not leave many people. All throughout life many a person battles the youthful passions that they have never run from. It may be that our mind might cause us to return to a youthful passion that is not holy and pure. In each of these events, Scripture compels us to run to flee. We are to flee just as Joseph did from Potiphar's wife in Egypt, **Genesis 39.**

Fleeing is not easy. Fleeing takes determination and consistency. Youthful passions do not just leave. They are reoccurring, and we must be on the offensive with our eyes wide open. The danger is that youthful lusts and passions do not go away or come to the point that they are of less concern. Youthful lusts begin in our youth. They are *"the lust of the flesh, the lust of the eyes, and the pride of life,"* **1 John 2:16 NKJV.** Never place yourself in a situation where they can be cultivated and grow into acts of sin. Lust is sin. You can always choose to run or leave a situation. Never feel you are above youthful lusts. *"Therefore let him who thinks he stands take heed lest he fall."* **1 Corinthians 10:12 NKJV**

If you are having a battle with youthful passions, consider the lyrics of this worship song by Candi Pearson Shelton, "One Pure and Holy Passion":

> *Give me one pure and holy passion,*
> *Give me one magnificent obsession.*
> *Give me one glorious ambition for my life*
> *To know and follow hard after you.*
>
> *To know and follow hard after you*
> *To grow as your disciple in your truth.*
> *This world is empty, pale, and poor*
> *Compared to knowing you, my Lord,*
>
> *Lead me on and I will run after you*
> *Lead me on and I will run after you.*
> **Candi Pearson Shelton**

"So flee youthful passions and pursue righteousness, faith, love, and peace, along with those who call on the Lord from a pure heart. **2 Timothy 2:22 ESV**

Think about it. *Selah!*

Day 24:
Tithing Is for Everyone

"Each one must give as he has decided in his heart, not reluctantly or under compulsion, for God loves a cheerful giver. And God is able to make all grace abound to you, so that having all sufficiency in all things at all times, you may abound in every good work." **2 Corinthians 9:7-8 ESV**

I have always wondered why it is that believers seem to struggle with the issue of tithing. We know that we are God's child, His messenger, and His servant, and that all we have is God's and came from His good hand. How is it then that we grapple with the thought of returning a portion of our allowance to our Father, knowing that He will give us even more?

Here are the truths in tithing:

1. We belong to God and we are His adopted children.
2. Everything we have belongs to God and came from His good hand.
3. He asks us to return 10% of our allowance to Him to put in the bank of heaven.
4. We all are able to meet His request, and we should do as He asks cheerfully.
5. He does not ask more than He has provided us to give.
6. He promises to give us more allowance if we return his 10%.
7. He promises to blow our minds with unbelievable blessing in our lives.

8. He promises us a greater return for our return, enriched in every way.
9. He promises to keep away from us anything that would prevent profit in business and in our health.
10. He promises to make us to be a blessing and profit to others and a desired friend.

"For the ministry of this service is not only supplying the needs of the saints but is also overflowing in many thanksgivings to God." **2 Corinthians 9:12 ESV**

Tithing is not just a way for us to experience the good hand of God, but that the world might also be able to see the good hand of God as well.

Don't fall into the trap of feeling you cannot tithe, because you can. Every person must make the decision in his own mind to give as God has blessed him and to give cheerfully. When we accept God's request, we then become the recipients of His challenge. Will you accept it? You are not only able to do this but you will greatly benefit from it. Don't wish that you had more money. Give to God as He has blessed you, and you will receive much more than you give. This is God's **"Quid Pro Quo,"** something for something, something great for something little. So, little is much when God is added to it.

"Each one must give as he has decided in his heart, not reluctantly or under compulsion, for God loves a cheerful giver. And God is able to make all grace abound to you, so that having all sufficiency in all things at all times, you may abound in every good work." **2 Corinthians 9:7-8 ESV**

"Bring the full tithe into the storehouse, that there may be food in my house. And thereby put me to the test, says the Lord of hosts, if I will not open the windows of heaven for you and pour down for you a blessing until there is no more need. I will rebuke the devourer for you, so that it will not destroy the fruits of your soil, and your vine in the field shall not fail to bear, says the Lord of hosts. Then all nations will call you blessed, for you will be a land of delight, says the Lord of hosts."
Malachi 3:10-12 ESV

Tithing is for everyone. There is no one who is unable to tithe, because God has your back. He stands behind His Word, and His Word is true. All you need to do to be a recipient of this blessing is to trust and obey.

Think about it. *Selah*

Day 25:
The Big Surprise

"This is my life work: helping people understand and respond to this Message. It came as a sheer gift to me, a real surprise, God handling all the details. When it came to presenting the Message to people who had no background in God's way, I was the least qualified of any of the available Christians. God saw to it that I was equipped, but you can be sure that it had nothing to do with my natural abilities."
Ephesians 3:7-8 The Message

A gift is something that you did not purchase, and it was given to you because someone appreciated you for some reason. A gift is a blessing which carries with it joy, but an unexpected gift carries with it unexpected and greater joy; it is a *"real surprise."* Expected gifts are not gifts at all. We feel as though we deserve them and are disappointed if we do not receive them. An expected gift is a payment, a consolation, or a compensation for fulfilling something. It is a participation trophy, and is not really worth anything.

When God gives us an assignment, a mission, or a ministry, He then fits us for it. He does not consider the obvious or what we have to offer Him. He looks at our offering of a willing heart.

- God's assignments reap a God profit.
- God's assignments go way beyond our wildest dream. **Ephesians 3:20**
- God's assignments render to God the glory and not to the one assigned.

- God's assignments meet the real need of people in a God way.

If you are capable of doing the assignment, it is not a God gift. It is a human gift. God doesn't empower the gifted. He gifts the ungifted with empowerment, and we are fueled by the Holy Spirit.

Paul says that his assignment was preaching, teaching, and writing about things that were way above his head, **Ephesians 3:8.** He said that he taught about the great plan of God that even the angels in heaven are talking about, **Ephesians 3:10.** He says that his ability was "not a brute strength but a glorious inner strength," **Ephesians 3:15,** a strength not developed but given, a supernatural gift, and a developmental asset empowered by the Holy Spirit.

What is your gift from God? What is your ministry, your work, or your assignment from God? Yes, God can use the natural gifts that He created you with, but He empowers those gifts to go beyond you to the point that you are not glorified but that He alone receives the glory. If you have any glory at all it is misdirected glory and must be corrected at once, **Acts 14:14-15.** What God does with you will be a big surprise to you and others as God gets the glory.

"This is my life work: helping people understand and respond to this Message. It came as a sheer gift to me, a real surprise, God handling all the details. When it came to presenting the Message to people who had no background in God's way, I was the least qualified of any of the available Christians.

God saw to it that I was equipped, but you can be sure that it had nothing to do with my natural abilities." **Ephesians 3:7-8 The Message**

Think about it. *Selah*

Day 26:
Creating A Clean Heart

"Create in me a clean heart, O God, and renew a right spirit within me."
Psalm 51:10 ESV

Eugene Peterson, in his paraphrase of the Bible, **The Message**, puts **Psalm 51:10** this way: *"God, make a fresh start in me, shape a Genesis week from the chaos of my life."* Did you notice the statement, "shape a Genesis week"? Do it again, Lord. Make me over and give me a new start because I have made a mess of my life. A golfer would say, "Give me a mulligan, Lord." That swing didn't count.

That is what sin is. It's a mess-up and a big mess. So, God actually takes our sinful being and recreates us. He makes us into a new creation. **2 Corinthians 5:17 & 21; Ephesians 2:10**

This recreation includes a de-creation. In creation God takes nothing and makes something, but in the recreation act, or de-creation, God takes something (sin) and makes it nothing. When God does that, it is as if it had never been. This act is not actually a "do-over;" it is an "all-new-over" creation. It is a perfect thing, and all the imperfections have now been made perfect "in Christ Jesus." **2 Corinthians 5:21**

Forgiveness is casting our sin into the "sea of God's forgetfulness." It is the blotting out or the degeneration, not just disintegration, of sin; therefore, making it nothing. Why? It is because God can't even look at an eraser mark. It must be nothing, or as though it had never been.

This is why God loves you. You are like His Son, Jesus Christ. When God forgives, it is gone! He creates in us a new heart, renews a right spirit, and restores us.

"Create in me a clean heart, O God, and renew a right spirit within me."
Psalm 51:10 ESV

Think about it. *Selah*

Day 27:
Authority

"Jesus came and told his disciples, 'I have been given all authority in heaven and on earth.'" **Matthew 28:18 NLT**

Have you ever been in a situation where someone attempts to lord themselves over you? You may think, "Who died and put you in charge or what authority do you have to do what you are doing?" These thoughts may run through your mind. Real authority cannot be challenged or questioned without a consequence. If someone has real authority, he has the indisputable right and power to give orders, to make decisions, and to enforce obedience. True authority has jurisdiction. It has command and control; it exercises dominance, sovereignty and supremacy over all. Authority solves questions, brings real peace, and gives confidence in carrying out a mission.

In **Matthew 28:18**, Jesus tells His disciples and believers today that the Father has given Him "all" authority in heaven and on earth. Eugene Peterson in his paraphrase *The Message* says that God authorized and commanded Him to commission us. There is no higher authority than God because He is supreme and He is sovereign. It is with this authority that He can give us confidence to do what He has commissioned us. It is with a full supply of provision and power on hand that we are sent. Our only valid response is to *Go* and make disciples. The mission will be successful because of the authority of the One who sent us. It is under His jurisdiction and control. We are His ambassadors and represent His powerful authority. If God is for us, then who has the authority to be against us?

What are you doing about the command of God? He has called you, sent you, and provisioned you for the mission. Are you going? You have the authority behind you.

"Jesus came and told his disciples, 'I have been given all authority in heaven and on earth.' " **Matthew 28:18 NLT**

Think about it. *Selah*

Day 28:
The Consulter

"When the Spirit of truth comes, he will guide you into all the truth, for he will not speak on his own authority, but whatever he hears he will speak, and he will declare to you the things that are to come." **John 16:13 ESV**

Advice and counsel, we seek it because of uncertainty. We find ourselves in a situation where we sit and wonder. We are watchful, we are careful and in control of our emotions, and we desire wisdom in the process of our decision-making.

"In the multitude of counselors there is safety," Solomon writes in Proverbs **11:14.** Isaiah tells us that Jesus is our Wonderful Counselor **(Isaiah 9:6)**. While Jesus was with His disciples, He was their advisor, counselor, and guide. When Jesus left for heaven, He sent the Holy Spirit to be our teacher, counselor, and advisor. *"When the Spirit of truth comes, he will guide you into all the truth, for he will not speak on his own authority, but whatever he hears he will speak, and he will declare to you the things that are to come."* **John 16:13 ESV**

When you want to know the truth, go to where the truth is found, the *Truth Storehouse.* Don't seek an explanation of the truth; learn the truth from the Teacher of Truth and the reminder of Truth, who was sent by The Truth. Don't seek opinions in life; seek the Truth of Life. People give opinions, but the Holy Spirit will "teach us all Truth." Opinions can be wrong, but the truth remains the truth in all situations. The truth can't be changed or altered because it is the truth. If you know the Truth, there is no need of opinion. The only thing left to do after the truth is found and understood is to take action.

In the book of **James** he writes: *"If any of you lacks wisdom* (needs advice and counsel), *let him ask of God, who gives generously to all without reproach, and it will be given him,"* **James 1:8 ESV.** He doesn't say God might give wisdom and guidance but that He <u>will</u> give it. What is confusing about that?

It's good to be able to have trusted, godly, and reliable friends but don't let them be the final "say-so." Let the Holy Spirit do what He is here to do and trust Him, not others.

"When the Spirit of truth comes, he will guide you into all the truth, for he will not speak on his own authority, but whatever he hears he will speak, and he will declare to you the things that are to come." **John 16:13 ESV**

Think about it. *Selah*

Day 29:
What Are You Fearful Of?

"And do not fear those who kill the body but cannot kill the soul. Rather fear him who can destroy both soul and body in hell." **Matthew 10:28 ESV**

I write this after the attack in Paris by the ISIS terror group on November 17, 2015. People everywhere seem to be in the grip of the unknown, uncertainty, and hopelessness. The problem is not the unknown of life but the unknown of death. We worry about life on earth because we are uncertain of what is on the other side of death. *"The thief comes only to steal and kill and destroy,"* we read in **John 10:10 ESV**. But Jesus has come to give us life and to give it more abundantly. Jesus is hope, Jesus is love, and Jesus is life. There is no fear in Christ Jesus. Fear is in this world, and it is fanned by principalities, powers, and workers of iniquity in heavenly places, **Ephesians 6:12**. We don't need to fear these powers but to *suit up* with the armor of God. That armor is more than sufficient for the battle. Jesus is also our anchor. He is our shelter, the protector of His sheep, and He is our sure hope.

Therefore he tells us in **Matthew 10:28** not to fear those who can only kill the body. Those individuals are earthly creations empowered by spiritual powers, but we are new creations in Christ Jesus and are empowered by Him. So, obey Him and trust His power. The terrorist is actually filled with fear and he wants to share that fear with us. Refuse it and draw near to God, and He will draw near to you. Resist the powers of Satan, and he will flee. **James 4:7-8**

The believer should not live in fear, but rather live, love, and rest in the arms of God. He holds your future, He holds your hand, He sustains you, and He loves you.

"And do not fear those who kill the body but cannot kill the soul. Rather fear him who can destroy both soul and body in hell." **Matthew 10:28 ESV**

Think about it. *Selah*

Day 30:
Have You Prayed About It?

"Do not be anxious about anything, but in everything by prayer and supplication with thanksgiving let your requests be made known to God." **Philippians 4:6 ESV**

I'm sure that you have shared a need, a desire, or a wish that you have had with someone to whom you had great confidence and respect and that person then asked you the question: *"Have you prayed about it?"* If you were at the point of sharing this prayer, it would seem that you had thought and prayed about it for quite a while. It also may be that you wonder if the request is selfish. The question may have come with just a passing thought, or you may have been talking with a friend who may have responded: "Well, why don't we pray about it or maybe you ought to pray about it." God is not only concerned about our needs but our desires and dreams as well. Eugene Peterson paraphrases **Ephesians 3:20** by saying that God is able to answer our prayers and meet our desires in ways well beyond our ability to dream. God answers our prayers in a "God way" not a "human creature way."

Praying about something is not demanding, commanding, or directing God to do something for us. It is requesting God to work in our life and to give us understanding as we live out our life.

The key in praying and making requests is that we don't get too anxious about the amount of time in the answering of our prayer request, but to be patient knowing that God is not bound by time but is bound by *His* timing. He does all things well and His timing is perfect.

Job had to wait. Abraham, Isaac, and Jacob waited. Joseph had to wait. Jeremiah had to wait. Daniel had to wait. Simeon and Anna waited for the Messiah, as did all Israel. Waiting does not mean that we will see the answer but that the answer will come. **Hebrews 11:13:** *"These all died in faith, not having received the things promised, but having seen them . . . ."* **ESV**

What am I saying? When we pray about things, we should pray believing with the understanding that God answers our prayers, but He answers them in "His timing," not in our time slot. God is patient and long suffering. He does not get anxious about anything; therefore, we ought not to get anxious. We ought to be grateful.

One more thing, God does not answer based upon our faithfulness but upon His faithfulness. *"Let us hold fast the confession of our hope without wavering, for he who promised is faithful,"* **Hebrews 10:23 ESV.** *"If we are faithless, he remains faithful – for he cannot deny himself,"* **2 Timothy 2:13 ESV.** Pray believing!

"Do not be anxious about anything. But in everything by prayer and supplication with thanksgiving let your requests be made known to God."

Think about it. *Selah*

Day 31:
What Do You Believe to Be The Truth?

"Then Pilate said to him, 'So you are a king?' Jesus answered, 'You say that I am a king. For this purpose I was born and for this purpose I have come into the world – to bear witness to the truth. Everyone who is of the truth listens to my voice.' Pilot said to him, 'What is truth?' "
John 18:37-38 ESV

I am sure someone has told you something you questioned in your mind, and you responded to him or her by saying, "Are you sure? Is that really true?" We often find ourselves in situations where we need to make a decision but we first must find out what the actual facts are.

What is truth anyway? How do you know that what you understand to be the truth is "The Real Truth'? Truth stands alone. It does not change for it is always the truth. If it is not the whole truth and nothing but the truth, it is not the truth; it is a lie. This is the foundation of information taken in a court of law. We state that what we bear witness is the complete truth, and is not tainted, and not altered in any degree or misleading in any degree.

Jesus told Pilate that He was the Truth and that He came to this world to bear witness to the truth as a credible witness. In **Revelation 1:5** John writes that Jesus is the one faithful witness to the truth. God cannot lie and His Word is the highest word and is an anchor, a hope, and a sure and firm belief, **Hebrews 6:13-19.**

If you or someone else is the anchor and foundation for truth, another person can challenge that belief as without credibility based upon that other person's credibility. But Jesus is the only true witness and there is none higher than He. How credible are you?

Pilate found no fault in Jesus based upon His word and the Roman authority, **John 18:38.** The crowd there overrides him and chose the credibility of Barabbas, who was a robber and murderer, **John 18:40.**

Therefore, if your truth does not match God's Truth, then your truth is a lie. Don't believe a lie. *"They traded the truth about God for a lie,"* **Romans 1:25 NLT.**

To know the Truth is to know freedom, to know liberty, to know peace and to live with the peace of God that passes all understanding because you "Know" the Truth.

"Pilate said to him, 'What is truth?' " **John 18:38**

Think about it. *Selah*

Day 32:
Perception or Vision?

"Now faith is the reality of what is hoped for, the proof of what is not seen."
Hebrews 11:1 HCSB

My Dad used to tell me: "Don't believe anything that you hear and only half of what you see." What he was saying is that what someone tells you is most likely undependable because it is secondhand information and polluted with bias; therefore, that information must be followed with personal verification. Also, when you witness something, make sure that it has not been tampered with by someone.

Here is the principle: Perception is how you view things as they are now. It contains no faith. Vision is a look into the future. It contains hope and faith.

How we view life will determine how we see our future. The future is seeing what is not visible, and it is the reality of what you have been hoping. If we go by what we see, there is no change. All things remain the same. If we remain the same, what we experience now is the best that will be, and our future will stagnate and decay. It is as it will be.

Don't stake your future by what you see now. Stake your future by what God sees and has prepared and planned for you. What God sees is beyond what you see and that is vision. If you allow God to be responsible for your future and you live your life with your hope and faith in Him, that faith then becomes reality. Your hope becomes fact.

Vision, then, is proven by the faithfulness of God and is not dependent on the insufficiency of my ability.

Think about it. *Selah*

Day 33:
How Can This Be?

Mary asked the angel, "How can this be, since I have not been intimate with a man?" **Luke 1:34 HCSB**

Have you ever asked yourself the question, "How did this happen?" Have you ever experienced a blessing from God's good hand and marveled at the reality that you have been the recipient of an unbelievable blessing? To say God is good is frequently used with blessings that we experience in our daily life, and this is true; but when something happens that goes against all logic and is contrary to all human understanding and thinking, we find ourselves in divine awe and wonder as to why would God do this. Why? It is because God desires to do so, and all things are possible with God. Yes, nothing is impossible with God. **Luke 1:37**

The truth is, what we see as awesome to us is simple and ordinary with God. Nothing is too difficult, too unthinkable, or too big for God to do. Big for us is little with God; but also, the little things we ask of God is no less little than the big things we ask of God. God cares about the little things in our lives as much as the big things. Man is little in relation to the universe but God's love for man is great compared to all creation. God cares for us! Nothing is too much or too little to ask of God because of His great love for us.

Never think that the possible is any more a bother with God than the big and impossible with us. All things are possible.

The Psalmist David thought about this and wrote in **Psalm 8:3-4 HCSB,** *"When I observe Your heavens, the work of Your fingers, the moon and the stars, which You set in place, what is man that You remember him, the son of man that You look after him?"*

So, Mary's thoughts were, *"How can this be?"* **Luke 1:34 HCSB**

Think about it, *Selah*

Day 34:
What Are You Worried About?

"Therefore, I tell you, do not be anxious about your life, what you will eat or what you will drink, nor about your body, what you will put on . . . your heavenly Father knows that you need them all." **Matthew 6:25 & 32 ESV**

We spend a lot of time worrying about tomorrow, don't we?

We worry about our job. We worry about family members. We worry about threats. We wonder about the future both near and far.

We wonder if we will have enough, and we wonder if we have done enough for the future.

We question the motives of others and their sincerity, their dedication, their motivation, and their dependability.

All the worry, wonder, and questions bring about anxiety in our lives, unnecessary anxiety for the believer in Christ Jesus. It is unnecessary, in that Jesus has promised to supply all our need according to His riches in heaven, **Philippians 4:19.**

He is our sure defense in time of trouble the Psalmist tells us, **Psalm 46:1.**

He has left the Holy Sprit as a Counselor, Director, Teacher and Comforter; therefore, to worry is to doubt and to doubt is evidence of little or no faith in what God has assured us.

Worry is a personal choice that we make as to how we will live our lives and worry only causes harm to the worrier, **Psalm 37:8.**

Wait and trust are the answer for worry. Wait on God to act in His own timing and trust His timing and His faithfulness to you.

What are you worried about? If you know how to give good gifts to your children and to others, don't you think that your heavenly Father knows how to give in the best way to you? Yes, you do and yes, He does.

Wait, trust, and be happy. Don't worry!

"...your heavenly Father knows that you need them all."
Matthew 6:32 ESV

Think about it, *Selah.*

Day 35:
Do You Think God Is Surprised?

"The Lord is high above all nations, and his glory above the heavens! Who is like the Lord our God who is seated on high, who looks far down on the heavens and the earth?" **Psalm 113:4 - 6 ESV**

God is all knowing. If God is all knowing, then world events do not catch God by surprise, and you do not take God by surprise. If you are the ambassador for Jesus, He has sent you where you are to do what He has asked. You are where you are by His will and in His full knowledge. This being true, make up your mind that you are going to be a confident, good and happy ambassador. Say what the King has given you to say. Don't add to it or take away from it; tell it as it is.

- God is your authority.
- He is your power.
- He is your credibility.
- He has your back.

If the people to whom you have been sent with His message do not listen or refuse to take the message seriously, they are at fault, not you. The ambassador delivers the message, and if it is refused, Jesus will take the refusal personally and will respond personally.

The reaction of those hearers has not taken God by surprise. He waits to give them time and is displaying His patience and longsuffering character to the world because He does not want anyone to perish. **2 Peter 3:9**

God waits because He is patient and because of His love for man, not desiring anyone would perish. What we perceive as an unexpected event in our life is totally expected in the eyes of God. The events of today may have us confused, but God is not confused nor taken by surprise. His eyes are open and perceptive but His heart is loving, kind, gracious and merciful. *"The Lord is in his holy temple; the Lord's throne is in heaven; his eyes see, his eyelids test the children of man,"* **Psalm 11:4 ESV.** God is patient, so He waits.

Remember, our job is not to convict and cause change, our job is to carry the Good News to those we meet. God is for us and has sent us. We must only be faithful and obedient.

"The Lord is high above all nations, and his glory above the heavens! Who is like the Lord our God who is seated on high, who looks far down on the heavens and the earth?" **Psalm 113:4 – 6 ESV**

God is not surprised; He is long suffering.

Think about it. *Selah*

Day 36:
Rejected

"He was despised and rejected by men; a man of sorrows, and acquainted with grief;" **Isaiah 53:3 ESV**

Rejection! No one desires to be rejected. No one enjoys being in the grip of sorrow, and no one wants to experience grief. Everyone will do all that is possible to escape rejection, sorrow, and grief. Depression is usually what follows rejection. Depression is the fruit of sorrow, and its thorn is grief.

Jesus told His disciples that they should expect trouble and should not be surprised by the rejection of others and not give in to grief. He offered an alternative to grief and that was good cheer because He has overcome the world. He said rejection is part of being His disciple. If the world hated Him, why would we expect anything else? We are not greater than He.

That is the bad news, but the good news is that He prepared for us a Helper, an Advocate or a Comforter, a Guide, and one who would walk alongside of us, a Paraclete. That confidant is the Holy Spirit, the third part of the Trinity that Jesus personally left with us and for us.

The old saying, *"misery loves company,"* is true but that statement carries with it the idea of sadness and no relief in sight. Jesus has born our sorrow. He has carried our grief and has invited us to place our burdens upon Him and to take His easy yoke upon us to aid in the carrying of our rejection, grief and sorrow. **Isaiah 53:3-5; Matthew 11:29**

The believer's life is one marked by rejection, sorrow and grief, but it is a life of faith, hope, and joy in the midst of the storms of life. The life of the believer is strengthened in joy, the joy of the Lord, and bathed in love, the love of God. The believer is described as an overcomer and more than a victor. He is a child and heir of the King. **Hebrews 11:1; Matthew 11:29; Romans 8:31, 35 & 37; 12:12; 2 Corinthians 1:10**

Those who have taken Jesus Christ as their Lord and Savior have a redeemer and a sustainer in the time of rejection, sorrow, and grief! Sorrow lasts only for a time, but our joy will last throughout all eternity.

Think about it. *Selah*

Day 37:
Don't Do It!

"Take heed that you do not do your charitable deeds before men, to be seen by them. Otherwise you have no reward from your Father in heaven." **Matthew 6:1 NKJV**

If you are worried about things, perhaps your mind is on the wrong things. Notice some things Jesus warns against, the "don't do it" list of Jesus that will give you trouble:

Don't do things for praise. People don't like self-righteous people.

Don't pray for praise. People don't like pious people.

Don't fast for praise. People don't want to be around sad people.

Don't make money your god. People don't like uncaring people.

Don't worry about your everyday provisions. People don't like worry warts.

So, just don't worry about tomorrow at all because it's still today, and God is not finished with you today. He has things for you to do today. Today is not over yet, so obey Him today. God desires people of faith today.

If you want your praise now, then, that is all the praise and reward you are going to get. Earthly praise is temporary. It does not last; it molds, rusts, and fades away. God wants the praise.

If you want eternal praise and the reward that goes with it for eternity, wait. Our praise-worthy God desires to reward you, and that is real and lasting praise.

Do what Jesus asks of you today and don't worry about tomorrow. Tomorrow is in His capable hands. Don't listen and worry yourself because of the influence of this temporary earth.

Jesus says, DON'T DO IT!!!!

"Therefore do not worry about tomorrow, for tomorrow will worry about its own things. Sufficient for the day is its own trouble." **Matthew 6:34 NKJV**

Think about it. *Selah*

Day 38:
This Is How It's to Be Done.

"But seek first the kingdom of God and his
righteousness, and all these things will be added to you."
Matthew 6:33 ESV

Did you know that the very problem that you may encounter has a sure resolution? **Matthew 6** begins by saying don't be like other people in their worship and in their stress in coping with life; that does not bring praise and glory to God. The chapter ends with seek God and His righteousness and all these rewards and their resolutions will be added to your life.

Jesus is saying: Don't worry yourself, don't worry other people, just ask God and honor Him. Jesus encourages us to make it our first priority in life to honor God and to seek Him. He will take care of all the details of life. All the blanks will be filled in by Him and in His perfect timing. Jesus tells us not to do anything with the aim of being seen by others and rewarded by others but to be seen by God and rewarded by Him.

Prayer is how one communicates with God. It is a personal thing between you and your God. Pray privately with your private concerns to God, and God will answer your private concerns publicly for His glory. As the believer lives his life in the righteousness of Jesus, people will take notice, and they will glorify Jesus for what He has done.

When great concerns come into our lives and we desire to spend extended times in personal prayer, we can tell other believers so they may pray with us. We may desire to spend time fasting, but just fast privately and not to be seen by others. God will take notice, He will receive the glory, and you will get an answer in His timing.

As you pursue your goal of being and doing what God has called you to do, you will find true happiness in life. As you carry out that pursuit, you will find that God supplied everything you needed and more from His treasure house in heaven through Christ Jesus your Lord, **Philippians 4:19.** Money is not your master; God is, and He has an unbelievable retirement plan and place for you in his Kingdom.

If you seek God first, then you will notice that He has already prepared for you, just as He provides for all the things needed for all His creation. If you seek God first you will also notice that He takes all your anxiety within His care as well. You will notice that as you turn your anxieties over to God, not only does He care for you, but He masterfully turns your anxieties into great joy.

The conclusion to the matter is this: There is God's way, and there is the way of the masses of the lost. Don't worry about tomorrow. It is in God's hands, and if you are also in His hands, you have no reason to be concerned.

"But seek first the kingdom of God and his righteousness and all these things will be added to you." **Matthew 6:33 ESV**

Think about it. *Selah*

Day 39:
Fitly Joined Together

"From whom the whole body fitly joined together and compacted by that which every joint supplieth, according to the effectual working in the measure of every part, maketh increase of the body unto the edifying of itself in love." **Ephesians 4:16 KJV**

I am sixty-nine years old as of this year, 2016, and I was taught by my parents to memorize Scripture from the King James Version. Although the translation is antiquated, I enjoy quoting those verses as I have memorized them from that translation. The newer translations and paraphrases speak more clearly to new Christians today and to those younger than I, but I still prefer to quote Scripture the way I first was taught.

The old English words of the King James Version in **Ephesians 4:16,** *"fitly joined together,"* are very descriptive to me. The church is *"fitly joined together"* by Christ Jesus to the special work that it has been established to do. *"Fitly,"* like in a puzzle where everything fits together perfectly and there are no cracks, holes or parts that have not been craftily planned and prepared.

"Fitly joined," where there is only one-way to complete the puzzle and that is by the workmanship of the creator. Pieces do not have to be forced into place. They just

come together when placed in the position that they were created and just the way the Master planned.

"Fitly joined together" in making one beautiful picture and all who see it are amazed and blessed by it. The church is the body of Christ, and He has prepared each person in His church as a special shape that joins together with the next piece. There is great unity there.

It is when we try to force our piece or another piece into a position that is contrary to the work of the Creator that we find stress, strain, and division in the church. So, do as the old Gospel song proclaimed: *"Brighten the corner where you are;"* but, if you are not a corner piece, you will mess up the whole picture.

Be happy where God has placed you and don't look at other pieces of the picture. You are that special piece that God has prepared for a very special place. You will not be happy anywhere else.

Enjoy being *"fitly joined together"* and everyone will be happy, and God will be honored.

"From whom the whole body fitly joined together and compacted by that which every joint supplieth, according to the effectual working in the measure of every part, maketh increase of the body unto the edifying of itself in love." **Ephesians 4:16 KJV**

Think about it. *Selah*

Day 40:
Are You Satisfied?

"And they all ate and were satisfied. And they took up twelve baskets full of the broken pieces left over."
Matthew 14:20 ESV

It is said that after James Butler Hickok, or "Wild Bill" as we know him, shot and killed Confederate Army veteran Dave Tutt in a street shoot-out in Springfield, Missouri, he said, *"Are you satisfied, gentlemen?"* What "Wild Bill" was saying was: "Is this what you came to see? Are you satisfied now?"

Satisfied. Life is made up of our efforts that come from not being satisfied, from a coveting of something greater and better. James writes in **James 4:1:** *"What causes quarrels and what causes fights among you? Is it not this that your passions are at war within you? You desire and do not have, so you murder. You covet and cannot obtain, so you fight and quarrel."* **ESV**

Not being satisfied can be a good thing if our passion is for the good of all; but too often our dissatisfaction is due to evil passions, coveting, and selfishness. This evil passion is greed, self-fulfillment, and is expressed in greed. Someone asked James D. Rockefeller: *"How much money is enough?"* His response was, *"Just a little more."* I think it is safe to say that is greed.

Yet, too often that is what drives many of us in our pursuit of personal passions in life. If we are to be satisfied in a good way, we must establish our passions and desires in a good way or upon a good individual.

Jesus reminded the rich young ruler: *"Why do you call me good? No one is good except God alone,"* **Luke 18:19 ESV.** He was rich, he was young, he had power and position in life, he was versed in Scripture and very religious, and yet, he was not satisfied. He thought that his feeling of dissatisfaction was a proper response. Jesus wanted to help this young man, and we find that Jesus' description of this young man was mostly positive. He said, "Young man, you only lack one thing." Jesus didn't tell him what that one thing was, but he drove it home to him by telling him to go sell all that he had and give it to the poor, **Vs. 22.** The conclusion was, *"he became very sad, for he was extremely rich,"* **Vs. 23.**

This young man came to the understanding that he was not willing to do just one more thing. He wanted one more thing. Like John D. Rockefeller, he wanted just a little bit more, and he was not willing to give up anything.

What about you? What is the root of your dissatisfaction? What is it that you are pursuing in your life endeavor? Are you seeking praise? What about power? Are you looking for a better position in life? What are you lacking and are you willing to give up anything to be looked upon with satisfaction in the eyes of Christ? Is Jesus satisfied with you? I like this song written by B. B. McKinney: *"Satisfied with Jesus".* Ponder these words for a moment:

I am satisfied with Jesus, He has done so much for me,
He has suffered to redeem me, He has died to set me free.
I am satisfied, I am satisfied, I am satisfied with Jesus,
But the question comes to me, as I think of Calvary,
Is my Master satisfied with me?

"Gentlemen, are you satisfied?" "Just a little more." Or, I am yours Lord, take me, mold me, use me, my life is in your hands. When your life is in Jesus' hands, He will take it up, bless it, and there will satisfaction with much more left over. He does exceedingly abundantly above all that you might ask or think, **Ephesians 3:20.**

"And they all ate and were satisfied. And they took up twelve baskets full of the broken pieces left over." **Matthew 14:20 ESV**

Think about it. *Selah*

Day 41:
One Step At A Time

"Now the Lord said to Abram, 'Go from your country and your kindred and your father's house to the land that I will show you.'" **Genesis 12:1 ESV**

Has there ever been a time in your life where God has given you a vision of ministry yet you question that vision? From where did that doubt come? Was it God? But you have acknowledged that God is the one who gave you the vision. Has God changed his mind? Why would God change His mind if He knows all things?

2 Peter 1:10 encourages us to make our calling and election sure that we might be confident.

2 Corinthians 4:1 tells the believer that it is God in His mercy that has given us the wonderful work of telling his Good News to others and with that knowledge and confidence and assurance, we should never give up.

Here is what I am wanting you to know: God does not give us the whole map. He is like a GPS. He gives us one step at a time. In **Genesis 12,** God called Abram to go to a place that He would show him, and in **Hebrews 11:8,** the writer reveals to us that Abraham did not know where he was going. Abraham only knew that God was going to show it to him. In **Genesis 12:7,** we see God giving Abraham the answer after he arrived in Canaan: ". . . I will give you this land."

The Wise men had to follow the star not sure of where it would lead them. The disciples had to follow Jesus unsure of what would happen, where it would happen, and they totally misunderstood when it would happen. They just followed Jesus. **Isaiah 30:21 ESV:** *"This is the way, walk in it."*

Joseph was unsure, Mary was unsure, Zacharias was unsure, the thief on the cross was unsure, and Philip was unsure as was the Ethiopian Eunuch, but their faith and their assurance was in the Word of the Lord to them.

When God speaks, believe it and go for it. Do not turn around. Do not delay. Just go and believe.

"Now the Lord said to Abram, 'Go from your country and your kindred and your father's house to the land that I will show you.'" **Genesis 12:1 ESV**

Think about it. *Selah*

Day 42:
I Am Your Shield

"After these things the word of the Lord came to Abram in a vision: 'Fear not, Abram, I am your shield; your reward shall be very great.'" **Genesis 15:1 ESV**

A shield will give the soldier confidence in the thick of battle. The Romans had many shields. The *scutum* was one shield designed for protecting the soldier from spears, javelins, arrows, swords and daggers. The *testudo* shield was another one, and it would create a shield wall giving the soldier protection from all sides. It would give protection against the many arrows and darts of the enemy in the open battle field.

Notice how faith and the shield are used. In **Hebrews 11:1 ESV** we read: *"Now faith is the assurance of things hoped for, the conviction of things not seen."*

In **Ephesians 6:16 ESV** the Apostle Paul writes: *"In all circumstances take up the shield of faith, with which you can extinguish all the flaming darts of the evil one."*

In **Mark 4:40 KJV,** Jesus reproves his disciples in the experience of the storm on the Sea of Galilee: *"... Why are you so fearful? How is it that you have no faith?"*

We could replace **faith** with **shield** and get a good understanding of **faith:** "Now your shield is the assurance of things hoped for, the conviction of things not seen." "Why are you so fearful? How is it that you have no shield?"

God tells Abraham in **Genesis 15:1 ESV,** *". . .'Fear not, Abram, I am your shield; your reward shall be very great."* Abraham seemed to have let his shield down and was struck by one of Satan's flaming darts of doubt. God soothed Abraham's wounds caused by the flaming darts of Satan and encouraged him by His presence: *"But Abram said, 'O Lord God, what will you give me, I continue childless, and the heir of my house is Eliezer of Damascus?'"* **Genesis 15:2 ESV**

Abraham's faith was increased when God encouraged him by saying in effect, don't try to figure things out, Abraham; just trust me. Have faith in me. We then read in **verse 6,** *"And he believed the Lord, and he counted it to him as righteousness."* **ESV**

Abraham's faith was waning with the whims of time. God was saying: Abraham, keep your shield up, keep your faith up. I am your hope and I am the substance of your faith. Just do what I say.

I think we, too, tend to get caught up in the tangle of time. We think things are not going as they should, when in fact they are going just as God planned them. Remember, God is not bound by time but He is totally all about timing. In the fullness of time, at the right time, and when it is time, God things comes to pass and God fulfills His promises.

If things seem not to be going well for you, take up your shield, keep the faith, and remember where your hope is anchored. It will happen, at the right time, in the fullness of time, and at the very best time. You can withstand those fiery darts of Satan; just remember your shield.

"After these things, the word of the Lord came to Abram in a vision: 'Fear not, Abram, I am your shield; your reward shall be very great.' " **Genesis 15:1 ESV**

Think about it. *Selah.*

Day 43:
Retail or Wholesale?

"having the eyes of your heart enlightened, that you may know what is the hope to which he has called you, what are the riches of his glorious inheritance in the saints, and what is the immeasurable greatness of his power toward us who believe, according to the working of his great might..." **Ephesians 1:18-19 ESV**

A new Ferrari or Lamborghini are sold for what the asking price is. The most expensive car ever sold was a Ferrari for over 38 million dollars. There is no wholesale price for a Ferrari. On the other hand, the car that is considered the worst car ever made is the Yugo. There is no genuine retail price on the Yugo.

All of us are looking for a good deal. We look for sale prices, reduced prices, wholesale prices and the bargain basement real deal. Personally, I am the sucker who always seems to just miss out on a great deal. We look for deals because we want our money to go further; but the best of anything sells for the top dollar.

I remember in the early 70's after Bobbie and I were first married, the "Hundred Oaks Mall" was the premier mall in Nashville, Tennessee. There was a store in that mall that had a sign in the window that read: **"Nothing under $50.00. If you have to ask what the price is, don't come in."** That place of business, my friend, was not a wholesale place. Everything was top retail. It wasn't bargain basement deals; it was high rise for sure.

I don't know about Bobbie, but I never found a reason to go into that store.

Did you know that Jesus does not deal with wholesale and bargains? He paid the highest price and did not ask about how much our sin would cost. Jesus didn't say, "Wow, I got a good price on that!" No, He did ask of the Father, "If it be possible let this cup pass from me; nevertheless, not as I will, but as you will," **Matthew 26:39 ESV.** He was saying, "I'll pay top price; I'll pay it all and in full." He paid it all for the believer, nothing but the top retail price. God goes exceedingly abundantly above all that we could imagine. He supplies our every need according to His riches in heaven. Top price. At creation God did not say, "I got a good deal on that." He said that it was very good.

It is also true that God has for us His best for our best, but He only gives according to the faith that works in us. Do you want God's best for you? Do you want the retail stuff or are you satisfied with bargain basement deals and flea market prices?

May I challenge you to look for God's best and seek His best that He has for you. I'm not talking about financial. I'm talking about ministry, I'm talking about being used by God to the utmost of His desire for you. I'm talking about the plans that He has for you, plans for your good and not for your harm.

Don't settle; strive for perfection!

"having the eyes of your heart enlightened, that you may know what is the hope to which he has called you, what are the riches of his glorious inheritance in the saints, and

what is the immeasurable greatness of his power toward us who believe, according to the working of his great might...." **Ephesians 1:18-19 ESV**

Think about it. *Selah*

Day 44:
Whatever Happens, Count Me In!

"Though the fig tree should not blossom, nor fruit be on the vines, the produce of the olive fail and the fields yield no food, the flock be cut off from the fold and there be no herd in the stalls, yet I will rejoice in the Lord; I will take joy in the God of my salvation." **Habakkuk 3:17-18 ESV**

This is one of my favorite verses because we live in a troubled world, and this verse offers tremendous comfort for believers. Habakkuk writes during a troubling time for his people. It is in this troubling time that he encourages us to make a choice, and the choice that he made was to rejoice in God despite his extenuating circumstances. He is saying that joy and happiness is the choice he has made and, therefore, he chooses joy over sadness. He is saying that the situation in which he and the nation of Israel find themselves does not take away the fact that God is good.

What is happening in your life right now? Have you lost your job? Have you been attacked by some disease? Perhaps a medical problem has appeared. Has your family suffered? Maybe a trusted friend or loved one has done something to disappoint you or perhaps even deserted you? Maybe your church is in a battle with individual wills and groups, and that struggle has caused a division among its members. Remember this: Whatever happens in your life, God is greater than that problem, and if you are in Him, remain in Him, and stay with Him, He will bring those issues to a good conclusion, **1 John 4:4.** Whatever happens you can count God in with you. Listen to Him and follow His lead, not others.

The next verse in **Habakkuk 3** reads: *"God, the Lord, is my strength; he makes my feet like the deer's; he makes me tread on my high places."* **Habakkuk 3:19 ESV.** The writer of Hebrews says in **Hebrews 13:8 ESV:** *"Jesus Christ is the same yesterday and today and forever."* **Malachi 3:6 ESV** says, *"For I the Lord do not change."* In this battle, this conflict, you can be assured that God is your strength and in Him you will not stumble no matter how difficult or steep the mountain may be before you.

What am I saying is, there is never a valid reason not to trust God for He has always been in total charge, and He will act according to His predetermined plan. You do not need to know the plan. You only need to follow him. Never allow the events of today and your situation to overcome you and cause you to doubt a God who does not change. His plan never changes. God doesn't change because He knew all things before He made His plan for you.

One more thing, His devotion to you never changes; therefore, be patient. Patience means you are in the grip of trouble. If you were not, then there would not be a need for patience. Paul tells us that it is the tribulation in our lives that works our patience, and God is at work in our tribulation, **Romans 5:3.** It is tribulation that gives us reason to glory and praise God because we experience the faithfulness of God in that time of trouble, **Psalm 46:1.** Trouble is where you gain strength and why you can be a help to others in their time of trouble. He is our shield or faith in the battle, so we can patiently wait on Him, **Psalm 33:20.**

Francis de Sales once said: *"Go on joyously as much as you can, and if you do not always go on joyously, at best go on courageously and confidently."* It is in Christ that we go.

"Though the fig tree should not blossom, nor fruit be on the vines, the produce of the olive fail and the fields yield no food, the flock be cut off from the fold and there be no herd in the stalls, yet I will rejoice in the Lord; I will take joy in the God of my salvation." **Habakkuk 3:17-18 ESV**

Think about it. *Selah*

Day 45:
This Is More Than I Can Bear!

"Come to me, all who labor and are heavy laden, and I will give you rest. Take my yoke upon you, and learn from me, for I am gentle and lowly in heart, and you will find rest for your souls. For my yoke is easy, and my burden is light." **Matthew 11:28-30 ESV**

Why? Why is this happening to me God? This is more than I can bear!

Yes, it is more than you can bear alone. "Come unto me," Jesus beacons to us in our times of being heavy laden. Bring your difficulties to me and let me help. Place those difficult loads onto my yoke and I will help bear it with you.

It is in the difficult times that we learn of God's all sufficiency, dependability, and power. It is in these times of burdens that we discover a rest, a time of refreshment, and a time to rebuild confidence for the task. Notice that Jesus doesn't say He would remove the burden but that He would make the burden light and manageable.

When I transfer my burdens upon Jesus as He asks of me, in my mind's eye I can see His smiling face and bright eyes as He lovingly picks up that burden of mine and eases my strain. I still have the burden, but it is so much lighter now because I am yoked to Him, and that burden is nothing to Him. As we walk together, He encourages me, "See, Danny, we can do it and when yoked with me, you can do all things."

When others see me at peace and coping with my perceived heavy burden they wonder: "How does he do it?" The answer is, I can't do it but, we (Jesus and I) can do it. It is then that He receives the glory. By the way, can you think of anyone in the Bible or in all of history, who did not experience, at times, some type of burden? Life is a burden for all, life is a struggle for everyone. Jesus took upon Himself the sins of the world. Just before He picked up that load of sin, He told His disciples that in this world . . . expect trouble, expect burdens. After that, He brought them some words of comfort when He said: *"But be of good cheer; I have overcome the world,"* **John 16:33 KJV.** He was saying He took the big part of the load away but, we were still to expect some.

It is a bit puzzling to hear, *"be of good cheer,"* in the same breath as "expect trouble." Henry Blackaby offers good advice: *"Don't resent the suffering God allows in your life. Don't make all your decisions and invest everything you have into avoiding hardship. God did not spare His own Son. How can we expect Him to spare us? Learn obedience even when it hurts."*

Why you? Because God is displaying to the world, through you, that there can be found a greater peace in the time of great trouble. They witness it in you and they begin to seek the God of all peace in their life. At this point you are being used of God and He receives all the glory.

"Come unto me, all who labor and are heavy laden, and I will give you rest. Take my yoke upon you, and learn from me, for I am gentle and lowly in heart, and you will find rest for your souls. For my yoke is easy, and my burden is light." **Matthew 11:28-30 ESV** Think about it. *Selah*

Day 46:
"Use Temporal Things But Desire Eternal Things"

"But seek first the kingdom of God and his righteousness, and all these things will be added to you." **Matthew 6:33 ESV**

"Things" . . . The adage is: "He who dies with the most toys wins." Do you believe that? We work to acquire "things," to have various "things," and even to devise intricate schemes for which we might obtain them; but not just any thing is worth having. Most things are temporary.

Thomas a' Kempis wrote in his book, The Imitation of Christ: *"Whatever I can desire or imagine for my own comfort I look for not here but hereafter. For if I alone should have all the world's comforts and could enjoy all its delights, it is certain that they could not long endure. . . .. If you desire these present things too much, you will lose those which are everlasting and heavenly. Use temporal things but desire eternal things. You cannot be satisfied with any temporal goods because you were not created to enjoy them."*

Jesus tells us: *"For where your treasure is, there your heart will be also."* **Matthew 6:21 ESV.** He also warned that for all our efforts for praise, recognition, or reward we may get on earth that is all we will get, **Matthew 6:16.**

It is natural to covet things. Adam and Eve coveted the fruit of the Tree of Knowledge of Good and Evil. This led to their son Cain's coveting of personal praise. Achan coveted money and the designer clothing of Shinar. On and on it goes, and throughout history we see that the misplacement of desire and the coveting for things has ruined so many.

When John D. Rockefeller, who was a believer in Christ Jesus, was asked how much money was enough, his response was: *"Just a little more."* When our desires are focused upon what we see here on earth, it means we have taken our eyes off Jesus and what He is preparing for us in heaven. It means that we have changed our aim in life and desire to acquire on earth and not to lay up treasures in heaven.

One more caution about things: Things tend to ruin our love for others. Things change our focus from God and others to self. When our "desire" is not to follow Jesus and obey Him but to follow a self-centered desire while disregarding all else, we have failed in our mission. It's about Him and them. Love the Lord your God with all your heart and your neighbor as yourself are the two great commandments.

Wanting things is not bad, but coveting them is another thing. So, what are the things in your closet? Are you a "trophy of grace" or a coveter of "things"? *"Use temporal things but desire eternal things. You cannot be satisfied with any temporal goods because you were not created to enjoy them."* **Thomas a' Kempis**

"But seek first the kingdom of God and his righteousness, and all these things will be added to you." **Matthew 6:33 ESV** *"For where your treasure is, there your heart will be also."* **Matthew 6:21 ESV**

Think about it. *Selah*

Day 47:
Does the Word Of Christ Dwell In You?

"Let the word of Christ dwell in you richly, teaching and admonishing one another in all wisdom, singing psalms and hymns and spiritual songs, with thankfulness in your hearts to God." **Colossians 3:16 ESV**

Does the type of music that is used in your church make you mad? Why are you mad? Did you know that music is a human and personal preference thing? The Word of God is the divine thing and the unchanging thing. Music styles have always changed, but the Word of God, on the other hand, is a divine and God thing and therefore never changes. When you worship, listen to the Word of Christ within you being expressed in worship, if it is Scriptural worship, and praise God together while letting God be glorified.

Though I greatly enjoy the old hymns, I also enjoy the new praise and worship music of today. I am aware that what I enjoy of the old hymns today, at one time were new songs.

Billy Graham has made this comment about music: *"Instead of complaining to your pastor (or anyone else), I urge you to ask God to help you be grateful for all music that points us to God, new or old. No, you may not like some of it, but others do and God can use it in their lives to encourage them and bring them closer to Christ. Remember: The old hymns you like were once new, and someone probably didn't like them either!"*

I like to refer to **Colossians 3:16** as the church musician's **John 3:16**: *Let the word of Christ dwell in you richly, teaching and admonishing one another in all wisdom, singing psalms and hymns and spiritual songs, with thankfulness in your hearts to God,"* **ESV**. The next verse says: *"And whatever you do, in word or deed, do everything in the name of the Lord Jesus, giving thanks to God the Father through him."* **John 3:17 ESV**

May I make a few observations here?

- If God's Word is "dwelling in you," you will not have a complaining spirit.
- If God's Word is "richly dwelling in you," you will have a thankful heart.
- If God's Word is the reason that you do things in "word" and "deed," then you can easily see that the Lord Jesus is the reason to be happy while worshiping with fellow believers as they genuinely worship Jesus.

Ask yourself this question: "Why am I upset about music?" Do the words of the songs glorify God and are they Scriptural? If they are Scriptural and they do glorify God, I can think of no reason for you to be upset. *"If possible, so far as it depends on you, live peaceably with all,"* **Romans 12:18 ESV.** Does the church exist to please you or to please God?

"Let the word of Christ dwell in you richly, teaching and admonishing one another in all wisdom, singing psalms and hymns and spiritual songs, with thankfulness in your hearts to God." **Colossians 3:16 ESV**
Think about it. *Selah*

Day: 48
Why Do You Call Me Good?

"And Jesus said to him, 'Why do you call me good? No one is good except God alone.'" **Mark 10:18 ESV**

Why would a good and loving God allow the evil in this world? Have you heard this before? I am sure that you have, and most likely you have had that thought yourself. The answer to that question is God is good and loving, but this earth and mankind are not good and loving.

This earth and all that is in it is cursed because of sin. *"The Lord God said to the serpent, 'Because you have done this, cursed are you above all livestock and above all beasts of the field; on your belly you shall go, and dust you shall eat all the days of your life. I will put enmity between you* (Satan) *and the woman, and between your offspring and her offspring; he shall bruise your head, and you shall bruise his heel'* (Jesus, the first prophecy of God's plan for redemption, the Messiah.) *To the woman he said, 'I will surely multiply your pain in childbearing; in pain you shall bring forth children. Your desire shall be contrary to your husband, and he shall rule over you.' And to Adam he said, 'Because you have listened to the voice of your wife and have eaten of the tree of which I commanded you, 'You shall not eat of it,' cursed is the ground because of you; in pain you shall eat of it all the days of our life; thorns and thistles it shall bring forth for you; and you shall eat the plants of the field. But the sweat of your face you shall eat bread, till you return to the ground (physical death), for out of it you were taken; for you are dust, and to dust you shall return.'"* **Genesis 3:14 – 19 ESV**

A. W. Tozer wrote in <u>The Knowledge of the Holy,</u> page 88: *"The goodness of God is the drive behind all the blessings He daily bestows upon us. God created us because He felt good in His heart and He redeemed us for the same reason."*

Jesus came to redeem mankind or to give him the option of a "do-over," or perhaps I should say "a new-over," by making him a new creation, **2 Corinthians 5:17,** and to destroy this earth and replace it with a new heaven and earth, **Revelation 21:1-2.** Mankind would be a new creation prepared to live in a newly prepared place, the new heaven, the new earth, and the new city for worship, the New Jerusalem.

All of that is to say this: Yes, God is good and God is loving. It took a good and loving God to make things right, and in His divine patience, He demonstrates His longsuffering heart. He will give mankind the time to choose God and a new life, through his repentance of sin, or to suffer the penalty of death.

Mankind and this earth are contaminated with the curse of sin and are ruled by the creator of sin, Satan, and his angels. All the disease, every natural disaster, and every act of wickedness and debauchery are the direct result of the curse of sin, **Romans 5:12.**

Bad things happen on this earth and they will continue to happen, but God has a plan. His plan is for our good and not for disaster. It is for hope for a good future with a good God, **Jeremiah 29:11.** God is not okay with the way things are on this earth, and that is why He has decided to make all things new, **Revelation 21:5.** Don't judge the goodness of God by the evilness of this sin-cursed world and its inhabitants. Judge Him by what He has prepared for us.

God is not only good, but God is love as well. The love of God reaches down to creation and offers to us new life, eternal life. Yes, God is good!

"And Jesus said to him, 'Why do you call me good? No one is good except God alone.' " **Mark 10:18**

Think about it. *Selah*

Day 49:
I Want You to Be With Me

"And he said to him, 'Truly, I say to you, today you will be with me in paradise.' "
Luke 23:43 ESV

Did you know that it is the holy desire of Jesus to have a close and loving relationship with you?

Andrew Murray put it this way in his book, <u>Jesus Himself</u>: *"Did you ever hear of a man loving another and not longing to reveal himself? Christ longs to reveal Himself, but He cannot on account of our unbelief."*

In **Revelation 3:20,** we read that Jesus stands patiently at our heart's door and knocks desiring us to answer His gentle knock. It is up to us to open the door and invite Him in. When we do, He comes in and communes with us, fellowships with us, and has a meal with us.

In **Genesis 3:8-9,** we read of the daily walk that Adam and Eve had with God. It was a consistent time. *"And they heard the sound of the Lord God walking in the garden in the cool of the day, and the man and his wife hid themselves from the presence of the Lord God among the trees of the garden. But the Lord God called to the man and said to him, 'Where are you?' "* **ESV**

God does not hide from us; He seeks us. We are the one who hides and we hide because we don't want our deeds to be revealed. Jesus told Nicodemus that it is because of the wicked deeds of people that they hide from the light lest their deeds be made known, **John 3:20.** Jesus wants to take our sins that He already knows about and give us His light and righteousness to make us as clean and spotless as He is, **2 Corinthians 5:21.** When we live in the light as He is in the light, we are anxious to meet with Him. We want Him to see us, to notice us, and to love us, **1 John 1:7.**

Yes, Jesus wants to know us and desires that we might know Him. This is His great desire. He wants to reveal Himself. Do you desire Him? It takes a believing heart and a trusting act of faith by you. Do you hear the knock?

Answer the door, allow Him to come in, and you will be assured of eternal fellowship with Jesus for you will be where He is.

"And he said to him, 'Truly, I say to you, today you will be with me in paradise.'"
Luke 23:43 ESV

Think about it. *Selah!*

Day 50:
A Steadfast Love

"Let your steadfast love comfort me according to your promise to your servant."
Psalm 119:76 ESV

To be steadfast means to be unswerving in purpose. It is to be firm, fixed, constant, settled or established, not changing, fickle, or wavering. A steadfast love is a love that can be counted upon and is free of legitimate doubt. A steadfast love brings comfort because it is as steadfast as the one loving. Steadfast love has a firm grip on the one loved, and it has been established by its consistency in the past. It is a love that has been experienced by many and the one needing love. It is near, not far away. It is ever-present and not to be discovered. It is a now love and a dependable love through the future.

You see, God is dependable, and He never changes. He is the same today as He was yesterday, and because of that truth He can be depended upon in the future, **Hebrews 13:8.** He is our helper, our hope and our very present help, **Hebrews 13:5-6; Psalm 46:1.**

A steadfast love brings comfort in time of storm because the comforter is greater than the storm that is being experienced, **1 John 4:4.** The only questionable thing in a steadfast love is when there is doubt toward the Lover. Faith in the Lover is the shield that is required by the one being loved. That shield of faith will quench any fiery darts of doubt that Satan and his warriors may shoot at the one loved.

It is when we take our eyes off the Lover and focus them upon the hater that discomfort invades our life. There can be no discomfort in the arms of God. God has promised us peace. Jesus told His disciples that they should expect trouble in this world but as we experience that discomfort, pain, and persecution, we are to remember that Jesus has overcome the world and all its struggle, **John 16:33.** "Peace I leave with you," Jesus said, so don't let your heart be troubled, **John 14:27.** If you begin to be troubled by the struggle of life, take your eyes off the struggle and look at the Lover. At that time, you will discover a great peace that cannot be described and a comfort that is needed.

"Let your steadfast love comfort me according to your promise to your servant."
Psalm 119:76 ESV

Think about it. *Selah*

Day 51:
Open My Eyes, Lord

"Open my eyes, that I may behold wondrous things out of your law."
Psalm 119:18 ESV

It is essential for the believer to know the Word of God well in order to determine what is a right path to take. When he finds himself in need of wisdom in a course of action or a position to uphold, knowing God's Word brings assurance and confidence in life. Insecurity comes into our lives at the invitation of doubt or lack of knowledge.

The Word of God is our sword against an attack by the enemy. It is powerful and cuts quickly and sharply through the enemy, going all the way to the bone. When it is combined with our shield of faith, we become confident, we are comforted, and with God's provisions we drive the enemy away. We can boldly stand in the presence of the enemy. We find the provisions of God wonderfully effective in the battle. What we experience is a wondrous thing to behold. We discover unbelievable things of God.

The Psalmist asks for God to open his eyes. He asks God to open his eyes that he might see the things that have already been put into action on his behalf by God. Because he did not see them did not mean that they were not there. He is asking God to help him to see what God is already doing.

There have been many times in my life that I have mistakenly felt I was alone, forgotten, and neglected by God, but that thought proved to be a lie. What I was needing was vision and clarity of thought. What I really needed was to see God and His good and wonderful hand presently at work in my life. I needed to be reminded that if God has said something in His Word, it is to be trusted and it will happen.

To see God is to experience real peace. Where God is, there is peace, and there is liberty and freedom. To see God is to see the wondrous things from His Word experienced in life.

"Open my eyes, that I may behold wondrous things out of your law."
Psalm 119:18 ESV

Think about it. *Selah*

Day 52:
Lord Give Me Patience And
I WANT IT NOW!

"Be still before the Lord and wait patiently for him . . ."
Psalm 37:7 ESV

My brother David and I were talking about a problem that we both have, and that problem is that we are both impatient. Oh, we want to be patient and we desire to be patient in various matters, but my brother put it best when he shared with me, "I'd love for God to give me the gift of patience, but . . . I WANT IT NOW!"

In **Romans 8,** Paul speaks of the strain of waiting on the Lord. Waiting is part of the believer's life, and it is part of life itself. Nothing comes easy in life, and anything that is of any value at all involves waiting. If it is easy, it's not worth the wait. If something is of value, then it is worth waiting for, and that requires patience.

The farmer must wait for his crop, the industrious person must wait for his product, and the salesman must wait for his sale. Parents must wait on their children, and in old age the parent must be waited upon by the child; and we all must wait upon the Lord.

Actually, waiting enlarges the time of enjoyment of that which was waited upon. We eagerly wait for the prized thing that we have fixed our eyes upon and dreamed about for such a long time, and when it finally arrives, the joy we experience is well worth the wait.

Isaiah 40:31 encourages us that waiting on the Lord brings renewed strength. It brings about miraculous results that go far beyond the human ability to obtain. **Ephesians 3:20** informs us that when God does things for us, things that He has promised or called us to do will go way beyond our ability to dream about. Waiting on the Lord is worth the wait.

So, what is it that you are anxious about? Is there something that you have been praying about for years, and you have not seen that dream come about? Well, may I encourage you to keep dreaming, keep expecting, and keep waiting because the Lord knows exactly how to answer your prayers in unbelievable ways. God is not far from you. He is near you. He is right beside you, comforting you as you wait.

Waiting on the Lord does not deplete our strength; it increases our strength. Waiting on the Lord does not discourage us; it produces endurance and increases courage within us. Wait PATIENTLY on the Lord, and He will help you NOW!

"Be still before the Lord and wait patiently for him . . ."
Psalm 37:7 ESV

Think about it. *Selah*

Day 53:
Doing the Right Thing

"So I find it to be a law that when I want to do right, evil lies close at hand. For I delight in the law of God, in my inner being, but I see in my members another law waging war against the law of my mind and making me captive to the law of sin that dwells in my members. Wretched man that I am! Who will deliver me from this body of death? Thanks be to God through Jesus Christ our Lord! So then, I myself serve the law of God with my mind, but with my flesh I serve the law of sin."
Romans 7:21 – 25 ESV

Doing right is not always easy, as a matter of fact it is much too often found to be the more difficult thing to do. It was C. S. Lewis who said, "Integrity is doing the right thing, even when no one is watching." Doing the right thing takes integrity. I read on a poster somewhere these words: "Integrity is choosing your thoughts and actions based upon values rather than personal gain."

What is it that you value most in your life? What is the true foundation upon which your integrity rests and your actions are based? The choices that you make in life will reveal what that foundation is. But even if your foundation is God's Word, it does not mean that you will always do the right thing because there is a war within you raging and struggling for control of your decisions, and that is your natural bent to sin. So, expect it, prepare for it, and engage it with the power of Jesus Christ our Lord.

The battle for doing right will not end until your earthly life is finished, but when it does come to an end, you will be found to be the victor through Christ Jesus our Lord. So, never give up and always seek to do the right thing at all times. Remember that even when you do make the wrong decision, it is never too late to do the right thing. Acknowledge what is right and what is wrong. Someone has said that we will never see what is right as long as we are happy doing what is wrong.

And one more thing, don't blame others for your wrong decisions, not even the devil. You made the decision; you chose the road. You must repent of the decision you made and turn around. Repentance is turning around. As a GPS system will acknowledge, "recalculating, recalculating."

Be strong, be wise, be resilient, and be persistent and undistracted. The saying is true, "Weak people take revenge; strong people forgive and intelligent people ignore." The world system is wicked, stealthy, cunning, and strong, but greater is He who is in us than He who is in the world.

"Wretched man that I am! Who will deliver me from this body of death? Thanks be to God through Jesus Christ our Lord! So then, I myself serve the law of God with my mind, but with my flesh I serve the law of sin." **Romans 7:24-25 ESV**

Think about it. *Selah*

Day 54:
Be Consistent, Be Conscious, Be Courageous

"Do not swerve to the right or to the left; turn your foot away from evil."
Proverbs 4:27 ESV

Bobby Knight, the flamboyant basketball coach of the Indiana Hoosiers, made this comment on discipline: "Discipline is doing what has to be done, when it has to be done, as well as it can be done, and doing it that way all the time."

A winning team will be one that is disciplined in doing the right thing and not giving up; they do not quit. They go until the game is over. All throughout the game they are found to be consistent in doing what needs to be done, and they are consciously striving to do just that. They are courageous in doing what needs to be done in opposition to the struggle in which they find themselves. They are victors and successful in bringing about the victory.

Success and victory come from a building process:

- A **successful** believer in Christ Jesus must be **disciplined**.
- A **disciplined** believer in Christ Jesus must be **committed** to follow the Word of God.
- A **committed** believer in Christ Jesus must be **conscious** and focused on the race.

- A **conscious** and focused believer in Christ Jesus must be **courageous** in his battle.
- A **courageous** believer in Christ Jesus must be **consistent** in his preparation for the battle and **confident** in his coach, the Holy Spirit.
- A **confident** believer in Christ Jesus is **victorious** in the battle.

"Do not swerve to the right or to the left; turn your foot away from evil."
Proverbs 4:27 ESV

Think about it. *Selah!*

Day 55:
What Is This Thing of Grace?

"and are justified by his grace as a gift, through the redemption that is in Christ Jesus." **Romans 3:24 ESV**

The Apostle Paul makes reference to his personal prayer for God to take away a "thorn in the flesh," and in **2 Corinthians 12:9** the response that he received from the Lord was: *"My grace is sufficient for you. . ."* **ESV.** It is Vance Havner who is noted as quipping: "We hear a lot these days about 'cheap grace.' It doesn't mean much to be a Christian. But salvation is the costliest item on earth. It cost our Lord everything to provide it and it costs us everything to possess it." Jesus told the rich young ruler to go and sell <u>everything</u> that he has in **Matthew 19:21**.

Grace is not a frivolous thing; it is a costly thing. Grace is not needed for anyone to receive riches or favor on this earth, but forgiveness of sin can only be obtained by an act of grace from God, which is a grace that only God can give. Grace is given because of His great mercy. Mercy is "not receiving" what you <u>deserve,</u> and grace is "receiving" what you <u>do not deserve</u>. God's mercy is great and His grace is sufficient, and nothing but the righteousness of Jesus will do. The sinful creation dies and the new creation is made alive in Christ Jesus. That is grace. That is the purpose of God's great grace.

In the Gospel song, "At the Cross," Isaac Watts wrote: *"Would He devote that sacred head for such a worm as I?"* Today we find those words omitted from our hymnals and replaced with the words: *"Would He devote that sacred head for <u>sinners such as I</u>?"* The word *"worm"* is offensive. Though the cross is offensive to us and our sin is offensive to God, we are not as obedient as a worm is to the will of God.

I found written in one of my Dad's notebooks these words: "I never liked to sing, 'for such a worm as I' until I saw an ugly worm transformed into a beautiful butterfly." I might add here that it is God who has given us the voice that we have, and He beams with pride when we lift our voice in praise, singing out to Him. As the worm transformed into a butterfly glorifies the Creator, so do we when we sing to our Creator with our transformed voice. It is the Great Creator God who worked this display of grace for us to observe. When God applies His mercy and grace to us and covers us with the righteousness of His Son, we become graciously new creations and acceptable to Him. Now that is grace, expensive grace, and it is God's grace applied. It is exorbitant, undeserved, and sufficient.

Think about these verses:

"In him we have redemption through his blood, the forgiveness of our trespasses, according to the riches of his grace." **Ephesians 1:7 ESV**

"and are justified by his grace as a gift, through the redemption that is in Christ Jesus," **Romans 3:24 ESV**

"Let us then with confidence draw near to the throne of grace, that we may receive mercy and find grace to help in time of need." **Hebrews 4:16 ESV**
Think about it. *Selah!*

Day 56:
Don't Be a Quitter but Admit It When You Need a Substitute

"Only let us hold true to what we have attained."
Philippians 3:16 ESV

I don't quit and I don't give up, but I do recognize when a substitute must be sent in. When a substitute is sent in, the player must trust the wisdom of the coach for doing what is needed for the team. If you have played hard and given your all, there will come a time when the team needs a fresh player.

Caring for people is a demanding game. It is challenging as well as rewarding, but it is a great challenge to be able to accept the fact that your time is over and you must come off the field or the floor for the good of the team. At that time, you must come to grips with the fact that *"having done all"* you have played well and been faithful to your assignment.

A good coach will instill within his players that even when a game is lost, if you have played well, you can be happy with your efforts and learn how to be more effective in the next game or how you can help prepare another teammate for the next game. As a competitor we run, we reach, and we strive to conquer, but the very best of the best will not play in every game.

Play the game, play hard all the way to the end, and know when you need someone else to come in. Be happy in knowing that you have done all you have been assigned to do, and having done all, you can proudly stand.

"Only let us hold true to what we have attained."
Philippians 3:16 ESV

Think about it. *Selah!*

Day 57:
Duct Tape

"But when Christ had offered for all time a single sacrifice for sins, he sat down at the right hand of God," **Hebrews 10:12 ESV**

This morning as I was out doing some errands I noticed a church sign with this message: *"People use duct tape to fix everything but God used nails."* I like that analogy, but the truth is that it was not the nails that fixed everything. It was His blood.

We read in **Hebrews 9:22 ESV** *". . . and without the shedding of blood there is no forgiveness of sins."* The Law required that the priest offer a blood sacrifice for the sins of the nation and people, but it was a continual thing that was done day after day though it was insufficient for forgiveness of sin. *"And every priest stands daily at his service, offering repeatedly the same sacrifices, which can never take away sins,"* **Hebrews 10:11 ESV.**

The work of the priest was actually helpless and endless, but when Jesus paid the price with His blood, it was over. *"But when Christ had offered for all time a single sacrifice for sins, he sat down at the right hand of God,"* **Hebrews 9:12 ESV.**

The believer can take comfort in knowing that all that is needed for God to cleanse us from sin was accomplished by his Son Jesus Christ on the cross and sealed with His resurrection from the grave. Now there is no further need of sacrifice because all that was needed was used.

I love the hymn by Andrae Crouch, "The Blood Will Never Lose Its Power:

"The blood that Jesus shed for me
Way back on Calvary,
The blood that gives me strength from day to day
It will never lose its power.
It reaches to the highest mountain;
It flows to the lowest valley
The blood that gives me strength from day to day
It will never lose its power."

No, duct tape is not needed. It was blood and not just any blood. It was the precious blood of the Only Begotten Son of God, Jesus Christ, that was necessary. It is His blood that is sufficient to cover your sin, my friend. It was for you that He came. It was for you that the sacrifice was made and there is nothing left that you can do to add to its sufficiency or duration. The sacrifice is sure, and it is sufficient. Your forgiveness is set, fixed, and permanent!

If you do not know Jesus as your Lord and Savior you, can come to know Him right now. Acknowledge that you need a Savior and that Jesus is the only Savior. He will take your sins and cover them with His precious blood, and it will make you as clean as He is. Why not do it now?

"But when Christ had offered for all time a single sacrifice for sins, he sat down at the right hand of God," **Hebrews 10:12 ESV** Think about it. *Selah!*

Day 58:
Forgiveness, Deserved or Undeserved?

"For all have sinned and fall short of the glory of God."
Romans 3:23 ESV

If we deserved forgiveness, why would God send his Son to die for our sin? We do not deserve forgiveness. That is why we receive mercy and grace.

I have heard it stated by various individuals that they do not feel they need to ask for forgiveness for sin. I suppose that they feel clean and justified for all that they have done in their lives. I am sure that those same people feel that others need forgiveness for deeds that they may have done against them. They feel justified, but in their eyes all others fall short.

Scripture tells us that everyone, past, present, and future, has fallen short of God's measure of righteousness. Forgiveness by God is undeserved, and heaven is beyond the grasp of mankind; but God is love and because of the loving heart of God, He has made the provision for all mankind to receive sufficient forgiveness for all sin through His only and righteous Son, Jesus. *"None is righteous, no, not one;"* **Romans 3:10 ESV.**

Yes, all have sinned, and that "all" encompasses you as well as me. I am so thankful for that all sufficient "all."

It was Alexander Pope who pinned these words: *"To err is human, to forgive divine"* (<u>An Essay on Criticism</u>). We must admit that to be human is to sin, for all have sinned. The goal of God for righteousness is unobtainable by human effort, but it is available by divine act.

We all need forgiveness, and it is all undeserved. It is Jesus who can make us to be a new creation who is deserving to go to heaven and be in the presence of God. *"Therefore, if anyone is in Christ, he is a new creation. The old has passed away; behold the new has come."* **2 Corinthians 5:17 ESV**

Think about it. *Selah!*

Day 59:
Desires

"Delight yourself in the Lord, and he will give you the desires of your heart."
Psalm 37:4 ESV

What is your greatest desire in life? Our desires in life determine what we do, what we think, and whom we wish to be around. What we desire in life affects and reflects what our future will be. Our near future, far future, and eternal future are all related to what our present desires are.

The pursuit of our desires will greatly determine whether we are happy in life. Our desires reflect our soul, and they display before others our inmost being. Desires can be good or they can be bad. Desires can be lasting or temporary. Desires do say something about us. In the book of **James,** we read:

"You desire and do not have, so you murder. You covet and cannot obtain, so you fight and quarrel. You do not have because you do not ask. You ask and do not receive, because you ask wrongly, to spend it on your passions."
James 4:2-3 ESV

What does it mean to delight oneself in the Lord?

- To delight in something is to desire it.

- To delight in something is to take joy in it.

- To delight in something is to gain peace by it.

- To delight in something is to spend time thinking about it, constantly.

When our desires are God's desires, He provides us with the ability to acquire that desire and enjoy it. When man gives us his desires and provides ways and means to acquire them, the path is difficult and when gained, we find them unfulfilling.

Jesus tells us that where we store our treasures, or we could say our desires of life, is where our heart is focused, **Matthew 6:21.** If our desires are focused only on this world, then they are like the world in that they will not last. If our desires are the desires of God and treasured in heaven, they will be lasting and eternal.

If our desires are the desires of Christ, they will bring us divine joy, and they will also benefit others. If our delight is in the Lord, then He will give us the desire of our heart and we will be happy.

What are your desires in life? *"Draw near to God, and He will draw near to you."* **James 4:8 ESV**

"Delight yourself in the Lord, and he will give you the desires of your heart."
Psalm 37:4 ESV

Think about it. *Selah!*

Day 60:
A Losing Battle

And he said, "Listen, all Judah and inhabitants of Jerusalem and King Jehoshaphat: Thus says the Lord to you, 'Do not be afraid and do not be dismayed at this great horde, for the battle is not ours but God's' " **2 Chronicles 20:15 ESV**

Did you know that God's Will is always done even when no one may admit it or desire it? The challenge for the believer is to know and do the will of God. But in our quest to seek and know the will of God, we must listen to the voice of God. To listen to any other voice is to stray from the will of God.

A great deterrent in following the will of God is the believer's own mind. Peter thought he was doing the will of God when he cut off the ear of the guard of the chief priest. Peter also proclaimed that he would always follow Jesus, and he was wrong. Peter challenged the words of Jesus and the will of God when he said that he would never allow Jesus to die **(Matthew 16:22)**. In response to this remark Jesus said, *"Get behind me, Satan!"* **(Matthew 16:23)**. Peter was not in the will of God here. Peter also told Jesus that he would never deny him, and he was wrong. Peter was telling Jesus that his own understanding of the will of the Father was God's will. He opposed Jesus here, and he was wrong.

"I believe this to be the will of God." Often, we hear these words proclaimed in skirmishes between fellow believers and within a divided church body. In the fray, the contestants both claim to be upholders of "The Will of God." Abraham Lincoln wrote these words to a friend after the loss of the Second Battle of Bull Run:

"The will of God prevails. In great contests, each party claims to act in accordance with the will of God. Both may be, and one must be wrong. God cannot be for and against the same thing at the same time." **Abraham Lincoln in a letter to Eliza Gurney on October 6, 1862**

The words of Lincoln are true. *"Both may be, and one must be wrong. God cannot be for and against the same thing at the same time."* To utter these words means that the speaker realizes that he may be wrong. To do the right thing and to do the Will of God means that you are willing to consider the option that you are going down the wrong road.

In **Isaiah 30:21 ESV,** we read these words: *"And your ears shall hear a word behind you, saying, 'This is the way, walk in it.' "* The right road is followed when we follow the right guide. Because you want to do right and want to do the will of God does not mean that you will always be in the right road. Don't put your confidence in your own wisdom or another's wisdom. Lean your ear to the gentle voice of the Holy Spirit who is our guide. We must be willing to admit that we are wrong in order to be in the right in path of life.

The Will of God is never up for debate or alteration, nor does it require the support of any. God's Will prevails, and it is up to us to seek it and follow, not lead.

Think about it. *Selah!*

Day 61:
What Is It That Motivates You?

"I glorified You on earth, having accomplished the work that You gave me to do." **John 17:4 ESV**

The dictionary defines motivation as: to insight, to impel, to give cause, drive to inspire to action. So, what is it that drives you or that inspires you to action?

All too often our motivation today is to be successful, to be admired, to be looked up to, to have all and more than we need, and not to have need of anything at any time. Our motivation seems to be things, to have stuff, power, and position.

The greatly admired, much read, and frequently quoted Francis of Assisi admonished:

"Blessed is that servant who does not speak through hope of reward, and who does not manifest everything and is not hasty to speak, but who wisely foresees what he ought to say and answer. Woe to that religious person who not concealing in his heart the good things which the Lord has disclosed to him, and not manifesting them to others by his work, seeks rather through hope of reward to make them known to men by words – for now he receives his reward and his hearers bear way little from it." **Francis of Assisi** - <u>Admonitions.</u>

Jesus told the crowd in **John 6:38 ESV**, *"For I have come down from heaven, not to do my own will but the will of Him who sent me."* The motivational drive that incited, compelled, and drove Jesus was to do the will of the Father who sent Him.

To understand and know the will of God in our life and to do it ought to be our drive. When our motivation is obedience in doing what we have been assigned by God, then we become genuinely successful, looked up to, and have all and more than we could ever dream **(Ephesians 3:20-21).** God is seen as the provider in our lives, and God is glorified in it all. As Jesus prayed to the Father, we too can say that we have done the will of Him who has called us.

What is it that motivates you?

"I glorified you on earth, have accomplished the work that you gave me to do." **John 17:4 ESV**

Think about it. *Selah!*

Day 62:
True Things

"And we know that the Son of God has come and has given us understanding, so that we may know him who is true; and we are in him who is true, in his Son Jesus Christ. He is the true God and eternal life." **1 John 5:20 ESV**

Thomas A Kempis writes:

"The Saints who are highest in God's sight are the least in their own; and the more glorious they are, the more humble they are in heart, full of truth and heavenly joy, and not desirous of vainglory."

Vainglory is an interesting word. Something that is vain is empty, worthless and hollow; it is of no value at all. Vainglory is glory that is false, unworthy of glory and praise. Vainglory gives no glory at all, and it is a lie. It is in no way the truth. True glory is achieved by being close to God. It is not accomplished by one's personal ability but by one's position in Christ. It is not about what has been done by the person but by what is accomplished through Christ Jesus. Genuine glory is rightfully given to God alone and shared with us.

Jesus said in **John 14:6** that He was the truth, the way, and the life. As Jesus stood before Pilot, He told him that those who love truth would readily see that He told the truth. Pilot responded to the testimony of Jesus with the words the entire world ponders, "What is truth?" And "Truth" it was who stood before him, yet he was unable to see it in that his eyes were focused on self-glory, vainglory.

Today we still ask the question, "Is it true?" or "Are you telling me the truth?" Things that are true are things that can be trusted and relied upon, and that is a glorious virtue. True things are things that bring stability, comfort, and peace to a person's life. Yes, all who love the truth recognize that they can trust the words of Jesus as being true and will give Him glory.

To be near Jesus is to share His glory, and we are humbled by that simple truth. It is like the gospel hymn proclaims: *"It is glory just to walk with Him."*

"And we know that the Son of God has come and has given us understanding, so that we may know him who is true; and we are in him who is true, in his Son Jesus Christ. He is the true God and eternal life." **1 John 5:20 ESV**

Think about it. *Selah!*

Day 63:
Honorable Things

"Finally, brothers, whatever is true, whatever is honorable, whatever is just, whatever is pure, whatever is lovely, whatever is commendable, if there is any excellence, if there is anything worthy of praise, think about these things." **Philippians 4:8 ESV**

What is an *honorable* deed? An honorable deed is a deed that is done out of sheer grace and mercy. An honorable thing is a right thing, a good thing, and is beneficial to the receiver as well as honoring to the giver. An honorable thing is a noble thing that is preformed from an attitude of goodness. It is done for the benefit of another and is done in a dignified manner and without a desire for personal benefit. It was Blasé Pascal who said, *"Noble deeds concealed are most esteemed."* To do something for the sheer honor of doing it and because it is right is most noble.

I am quite sure that you have been the recipient of some deed or gift that was totally unexpected and puzzled you as to why? It is those gifts that are never forgotten and always brings joy.

Have you ever done something extravagant and unexpected for someone? Random acts of kindness display the love of God to the receiver. Random acts of kindness are also a blessing to the one performing that act. They are acts that are done "just because."

So here is my admonition to you: If you are burdened by something that has unexpectedly entered your life, think about those noble acts of kindness in which you have been the recipient. Take time to do something unexpected for someone, do a random act of kindness, and I feel certain that the burden in your life will flee. When we perform acts of grace, the Grace of God will overtake the burden we had, and we will discover that His Grace is sufficient for the suffering, **2 Corinthians 12:9**

There is a feeling of nobility that comes upon us when we do something just because we can, in spite of or in disregard of whom the recipient happens to be. Isn't that why Jesus did things?   Love your neighbor as yourself, love your enemies, and do good to those who despitefully use you. Do good, just because it is an honorable thing.

"Finally, brothers, whatever is true, whatever is honorable . . . think about these things." **Philippians 4:8 ESV**

Think about it. *Selah!*

Day 64:
Just Things

"Finally, brothers, whatever is true, whatever is honorable, whatever is just, whatever is pure, whatever is lovely, whatever is commendable, if there is any excellence, if there is anything worthy of praise, think about these things." **Philippians 4:8 ESV**

God is a just God, and He expects His followers to be just in all that they do in life. Justice is something that only God can give, but we can seek to live a just life and be involved in those things that are just in life. A just God desires that His followers live lives in a just manner. We are to be holy as God is holy **(1 Peter 1:16).**

What are just things? Just things are Godly things, they are righteous things, and they are pure things. To sum it up, just things are the things of Christ. Just things are acceptable to God because they reflect a righteous God. The believer has been declared righteous because the righteousness of Christ is poured over him to make him a new creation **(2 Corinthians 5:17 & 21 ESV).**

Just things are highly regarded things or things that are respectable and prestigious. Just things can be trusted and are things in which people can place their confidence. So, when we think and meditate upon those things, we have a sense of peace in our lives. Thinking about just things is to think about Godly things for there is none higher, more highly respected, nor more prestigious than He.

One of the greatest thoughts that a believer can have is that God is just to forgive our sin and count us worthy to stand before Him and live forever with Him. I love this worship Song "Before the Throne of God Above" written by Vikki Cook and Charitie Lees Bancroft:

"When Satan tempts me to despair
And tells me of the guilt within;
Upward I look and see Him there
Who made an end of all my sin.

Because the sinless Savior died
My sinful soul is counted free;
*For God the **just** is satisfied*
To look on Him and pardon me,
To look on Him and pardon me."

When Satan brings despair into your life, think about the just act of God made just for you.

"Finally, brothers . . . if there is anything worthy of praise, think about these things." **Philippians 4:8 ESV**

Think about it. *Selah!*

Day 65:
Pure Things

"Finally, brothers, whatever is true, whatever is honorable, whatever is just, whatever is pure, whatever is lovely, whatever is commendable, if there is any excellence, if there is anything worthy of praise, think about these things." **Philippians 4:8 ESV**

100% pure gold is gold that has no foreign matter in it. That is the best. When we think of things that are pure, we are thinking about those things that are highly treasured. When we think about pure things we are thinking about things of value and are treasured above all other things.

The real test of true purity is to place that which is thought to be pure beside that which is pure. Thomas a Kempis wrote:

"Purity and simplicity are the two wings with which man soars above the earth and all temporary nature. Simplicity is in the intention, purity in the affection; simplicity turns to God; purity unites with and enjoys him."
Thomas a Kempis

Josh McDowell has defined purity as *"Living by original design."* The creation of God can only be pure in that He is pure, but when sin entered God's creation, God's pure creation became tainted and impure. God is the test of purity and to test our purity we must place them next to Him. Only God can give us pure thoughts, pure desires and pure things.

Pure things are clean; pure things are praise-worthy; pure things bring joy to our life and are enjoyed without fear. I love the praise and worship song <u>Give Me A Pure and Holy Passion</u> by Candi Pearson because it gives a good picture of pure things:

"Give me a pure and holy passion,
Give me one magnificent obsession,
Give me one glorious ambition for my life
To know and follow hard after You."

That is what pure things are. Pure things give us drive in life and they are holy. Pure things are obsession in our lives that are huge and consume us. Pure things are ambitions in life that glorify God. Pure things are those things that compel us to be faithful, consistent and committed in desire to please God; to obey God's call in our lives and to have that God empowered drive to patiently and joyfully follow Him.

"... if there is any excellence, if there is anything worthy of praise, think about these things." **Philippians 4:8 ESV**

Think about it. *Selah*

Day 66:
Lovely Things

"Finally, brothers, whatever is true, whatever is honorable, whatever is just, whatever is pure, whatever is lovely, whatever is commendable, if there is any excellence, if there is anything worthy of praise, think about these things." **Philippians 4:8 ESV**

Things that are lovely are things that are worthy of being loved, admired and desired. Things that are lovely are precious and pleasant to be remembered and thought about. Lovely things bring a smile to our face. Lovely things are treasured things.

The old mountain Gospel Song, <u>Precious Memories</u> written by J. B. F. W. Wright, is a favorite of many.

> *"Precious memories, how they linger,*
> *How they ever flood my soul,*
> *In the stillness of the midnight,*
> *Precious, sacred scenes unfold."*

"Precious, sacred scenes unfold." Those are lovely thoughts that are so precious to our hearts that we consider them sacred and treasured. To think of things such as those cause the turmoil of everyday life to leave and bring peace.

The Psalmist David writes in **Psalm 139:17** *"How precious are your thoughts to me O God! How vast is the sum of them."* **ESV**

The Apostle John writes of some lovely thoughts in **1 John 3:1** *"See what kind of love the Father has given to us, that we should be called children of God.;"*

Jesus told his disciples in **John 15:15** that He no longer refers to them as servants but as "FRIENDS". And as a friend He shares His desires and mission personally with them.

In **Psalm 56:8** we read that God's love for us is so great that he actually counts each tear that we shed and treasures them with such great love that, he puts them in a bottle. How lovely is that thought!

Yes, lovely thoughts bring peace, they bring smiles and they cause us to open the treasure box of our mind to recount again of the many blessing and great love that God has for us. As we remember His provision, the thoughts we had that troubled our mind, just simply vanish away. Precious memories, how they linger.

"...think about these things." **Philippians 4:8 ESV**

Think about it. *Selah!*

Day 67:
Things of Good Report

"Finally, brothers, whatever is true, whatever is honorable, whatever is just, whatever is pure, whatever is lovely, whatever is commendable, if there is any excellence, if there is anything worthy of praise, think about these things." **Philippians 4:8 ESV**

A letter from a seldom seen family member or friend is eagerly awaited. When the eagerly awaited letter comes, it is read and reread over and over. The letter brings us up to date as to what has been happening to that treasured friend. That letter causes us to recount the pleasant things that we shared together in the past. That letter also gives us hope for renewed fellowship in the future. Good News brings joy to the weary soul.

If our health seems to be failing and we go to the doctor and he or she makes a lot of tests to find out what the problem is, we eagerly await the report of their findings. We are overjoyed when we receive a "good report".

As a child, we would proudly have displayed a good "report card" for all to see. We enjoy a good report for a good report makes us feel good about the work and struggle that we have had to endure. A good report is a commendation of approval and it gives us a greater desire to carry on to bigger and greater things.

Solomon presents a word picture of good news: *"Like cold water to a thirsty soul, so is good news from a far country."* **Proverbs 25:25 ESV**

The believer in Christ Jesus has been given has a personal letter of Good News to present to this vast world that is in need of Good News. This Good News is from a far-off country that offers peace, joy, forgiveness and hope for their future. This Good News is in your hands. Have you been delivering it? Don't hold back this Good News from this world of those in great need of a Good Report. If there is any thing that is worth reading, read the Good Report that is the Good News. That report contains Good News to all People.

The shepherds in the field heard the heavenly host proclaiming: *"And the angel said to them, 'fear Not, for behold I bring you good news of great joy that will be for all the people.'"* **Luke 2:10 ESV**

". . . whatever is commendable, if there is any excellence, if there is anything worthy of praise, think about these things." **Philippians 4:8 ESV**

Think about it. *Selah!*

Day 68:
Virtuous Things

"Finally, brothers, whatever is true, whatever is honorable, whatever is just, whatever is pure, whatever is lovely, whatever is commendable, if there is any excellence, if there is anything worthy of praise, think about these things." **Philippians 4:8 ESV**

Virtuous things are excellent things. Virtue is excellence, pure and respected and profitable. We are always in search of things of excellence. Excellent things are rare things, they are things well above the normal, the good and into the best things. Solomon speaks of excellent and virtuous things as those things of great values and wealth: *"An excellent wife who can find? She is far more precious than jewels."* **Proverbs 31:10 ESV**

Our everyday life is filled with everyday things. These thoughts of common things cause common worry, fret, strife and the common distractions, which keep us from enjoying life, as we should.

So my challenge to you today is to focus on the quest for excellence. Consider the virtuous things in your life which God has placed there. Think about those things and enjoy your life in Christ.

, if there is any excellence, if there is anything worthy of praise, think about these things." **Philippians 4:8 ESV**

Think about it. *Selah!*

Day 69:
Praise-worthy Things

"Finally, brothers, whatever is true, whatever is honorable, whatever is just, whatever is pure, whatever is lovely, whatever is commendable, if there is any excellence, if there is anything worthy of praise, think about these things." **Philippians 4:8 ESV**

"Know that the Lord, he is God! It is he who made us, and we are his; we are his people, and the sheep of his pasture. Enter his gates with thanksgiving, and his courts with praise! Give thanks to him; bless his name! For the Lord is good his steadfast love endures forever, and his faithfulness to all generations." **Psalm 100: 3 – 8 ESV**

Being "worthy of praise" means that a good, gracious, merciful and loving deed has been accomplished. In **Revelation 4:11** we see a vast number of worshipers standing before the Throne of God and all giving praise to the Lamb of God for it is acknowledged that He is the only worthy one for such praise. Such praise is reserved exclusively for Him, God's Only Begotten Son, The Lamb of God Jesus Christ.

To be worthy of praise is a badge of honor. But who offers the praise why they are praised determines the genuineness and worthiness of the praise. God is to be honored because he is worthy of highest praise.

Now, in **Philippians 4:8** we are admonished to think about things what are worthy of praise. What happens when we think of those things? Our minds are taken away from those things that have consumed our thought life. When our focus is turned on to the blessings of God to us and the greatest blessing of God for us praise erupts. We find the joy of the Lord consuming our thought life and we are happy in the Lord.

". . . if there is anything worthy of praise, think about these things."
Philippians 4:8 ESV

Think about it. *Selah!*

Day 70:
Fullness of Time

"But when the fullness of time had come, God sent forth his Son, born of woman, born under the law, to redeem those who were under the law, so that we might receive adoption as sons." **Galatians 4:4 ESV**

Is it time yet? No, it's not time yet. I am sure that you have been asked that question by a child and you in turn have responded to it with: No, It is not time. Just be patient, it's going to happen.

Though grown up I still have the question I ask myself: What's happening? What's holding it up, or they should be here by now. Times of perceived urgency still seem to fill our lives. Our prayer life frequently contains urgent request that cause us stress and great concern. We present to God our request that we feel God must take immediate and positive action.

Urgent things are those things where the outcome is doubtful or unknown to us. But there is nothing that happens or might happen where God is in doubt and all that He does is done well. **Mark 7:37**

Urgent things are pressing things; they are things that call for haste. Yet, God is not hasty in anything nor is He pressured to action before He intends to do so. Rather, God is patient in all that He does and allows all the time needed for everything to be completed in His pre-designed will. **2 Peter 3:9** tells us that God is patient and allows His great Mercy and Grace to be filtered into everyone because He is not willing that anyone would not have enough time to turn to Him. God does not want anyone to perish because of not enough time.

Hebrews 13:8 comforts the believer by reminding us that Jesus is consistent, and dependable as well as reliable at all times. He has proved it in the past, is, even as we speak, acting in our behalf and will continue to do so.

Yes, God is not hasty, He is perfect, all knowing and sure. His actions come only in the "fullness of time" **Galatians 4:4**

How does this relate to you and me? It means that we can be confident that God hears our prayer; that His actions for us have been planned for us before we even realized we had a need. It means that at just the right time, in the nick of time, the appropriate best action will fulfill our need and we will see it answered.

Remember, God is not bound by time but His Timing binds him. God is all about timing. He does all things well!

"But when the fullness of time had come, God sent forth his Son, born of woman, born under the law, to redeem those who were under the law, so that we might receive adoption as sons." **Galatians 4:4 ESV**

Think about it. *Selah!*

Day 71:
He Is Alive!

"He is not here but is risen. Remember how he told you while he was still in Galilee?"
Luke 24:6 ESV

Living proof. That is a statement that we make to declare that something is an undeniable proof of validity. After the death of Jesus on the cross we see the ladies coming to the cross with prepared spices to anoint the "dead" body of Jesus. But when they arrived the noticed that the huge stone in front of the tomb had been removed. This event caused them great confusion. As they looked inside the tomb, the body was not there. Where was the body?

It seems as though this should have jogged their memory. They had forgotten and needed to be reminded. What they forgot was what caused all the confusion in their lives. Jesus was continually telling everyone that He was supposed to be crucified and then on the third day He would come back to life. But they did not remember. It seemed that the events that had just happened overshadowed reality in their lives.

They saw the proof but did not remember what the fact which the evidence revealed. It took the statement of two men in "dazzling apparel" to shock them and bring their memory back. *"While they were perplexed about this, behold two men stood by them in dazzling apparel. And as they were frightened and bowed their faces to the ground, the men said to them, 'Why do you seek the living among the dead? He is not here, but has risen. Remember how he told you, while he was still in Galilee, that the Son of Man must be delivered into the hands of sinful men and be crucified and on the third day rise."* **Luke 24:4 – 8 ESV**

Sometimes we fail to see the living proof when it is right before our eyes. I think this happens many times still today. Jesus has said that He will supply all our needs according to His riches in heaven. **Philippians 4:19** He tells us that when He calls us to do something that means we can do it because it is He Who is calling us. Still we question, still we sit perplexed. We think we have come prepared, as the ladies had come prepared to do what was not needed, that which we have brought is not needed. What is needed and was needed at that time was "remembering what Jesus said to us".

So, remember that it is He who has called us; not us or anyone else.

- Remember in Him we can do all things. **Philippians 4:19**

- Remember nothing is impossible for God and if we are in God and God is in us; it is God who is doing the work through us. **Philippians 2:13**

- Remember He is alive and He is in us. **John 17:21**

"Remember how he told you while he was still in Galilee?" **Luke 24:6 ESV**

Andrew Murray wrote: *"A dead Christ I must do everything for, a living Christ does everything for me."* Jesus is alive! Remember! Think about it. *Selah!*

Day 72:
Friendship

"We exhort each one of you and encouraged you and charged you to walk in a manner worthy of God, who calls you into his own kingdom and glory."
1 Thessalonians 2:12 ESV

A person is known but the company he keeps the adage goes. Those individuals in ones life that go by the title of "friend" says much about the person. A friend is that is well knows by someone. A friend is kind, loving and resourceful. A friend is quick to enter into struggles with you. A friend is esteemed, can be called upon at anytime and in any situation. In a friend brings with him comfort, peace, support, and encouragement. A friend will never leave you. A friend is a blessing.

Not everyone has friends and few there are who have a close friend or a real friend. I love to read **John 12 – 17** where Jesus calls His disciples "friends". He was a real friend to them for He would not desert them, He would die for His friends. Jesus chose them as His friends and He went out determined to provide for them as His friends. He displayed Himself as a friend even to Judas who would betray Him.

It is this Jesus Who calls you His friend as well and wants to be your Friend. Yes, He really does want to be your friend. We do not deserve to be His friend but He makes us worthy to be counted as His friend before His Father. **2 Corinthians 5:21** One more thing, you can count on Him as your faithful Friend.

Jesus is an exhorter and encourager and supplies all your need is serving Him. He is worthy to be followed, proven to be trusted and there with you in time of need. Jesus is a real Friend.

So, here is my question: Do you want Him as your Friend? He died for you, are you willing to lay down your life for this friend? To what extent are you willing to obey Him as your Friend? I feel that your answer to each of these questions is yes. But here is what I would ask that you do; examine your commitment to your Friend.

One more question: Are you a friend to others? Are you an encouragement to others around you? Are you an example for others around you to follow? If so, you are a good friend and one to be treasured. You are a reflection of Christ.

"We exhort each one of you and encouraged you and charged you to walk in a manner worthy of God, who calls you into his own kingdom and glory."
1 Thessalonians 2:12 ESV

Think about it. *Selah!*

Day 73:
Hindrances, Oppositions and Conflicts

"because we wanted to come to you-I Paul, again and again-but Satan hindered us For what is our hope or joy or crown of boasting before our Lord Jesus at his coming? Is it not you? for you are our glory and joy." **1Thessalonians 2:18 & 19 ESV**

Have you ever felt hindered in your pursuit to live the Christian life as you desire? Does it seem to you that everyone is actively and aggressively engaged in making your effort difficult? Why is it that you are met with conflicts in your pursuit to serve Christ Jesus? The why can be answered in one word: Satan's forces of evil that abounds in our world.

The truth is we must expect hindrances; we must acknowledge the open opposition to our desire to serve Christ Jesus; and we must believe the inevitability of conflict to our service to Christ is upon us and will always be there. But the joy is this: That as we are hindered, opposed and are being stood against we are invincible in our performance of our calling, God's will for us. Did you know that though God's will can be opposed and conflict may be present in the performing of that will, it cannot be defeated? The conclusion of the matter is that we are already victors in Christ Jesus our Lord.

Have you read Fox's Book of Martyrs? John Fox was born at Boston, in Lincolnshire, England in 1517. He was a brilliant man a student of Scripture and Church history.

He is famous for his book: <u>Foxes Book of Martyrs</u>. He lived during the re-establishment of the Inquisitions of the Catholic Church in July of 1542, as a Counter-Reformation by Pope Paul III and continued after his death by his successor, Pope Paul IV. The Arch Bishop of Canterbury, Cardinal Reginald Pole felt it his sacred duty to *"Rid England and Wales of heretics."* "Queen Mary "Bloody Mary" executed, burned at the stake, 274 Protestants and it was at this time that John Fox lived.

This classic book is evidence that God is present though things may seem dismal in the believers lives; they were victorious. Though burned at the stake and suffered unbelievable atrocities committed by their oppressors, though they were hindered in the hour of conflict, God's will, was carried out by these determined men and women. The effect of this great oppression brought about change in God's timing, God's will, was done.

"I tell you my friends, do not fear those who kill the body, and after that have nothing more that they can do. But I will warn you whom to fear: fear him who, after he has killed, has authority to cast into hell. Yes, I tell you, fear him!" **Luke 12:4 & 5 ESV**

Our time on earth is but for a moment but life with Christ is eternal. Seek the eternal things. Judge by that which will last forever. The challenge is to let each believer lay up for yourselves treasures in heaven and do not be alarmed by hindrances, oppositions and conflicts today. Those things are pauses in our way they are not the end of our way. There is no end in eternity. The joy and glory in life is in the doing of what we have been given to do.

"because we wanted to come to you-I Paul, again and again-but Satan hindered us. For what is our hope or joy or crown of boasting before our Lord Jesus at his coming? Is it not you?   for you are our glory and joy." **1Thessalonians 2:18 & 19 ESV**

Think about it. *Selah!*

Day 74:
The Triumphant Entry

"So they took branches of palm trees and went to meet him, carrying out, 'Hosanna! Blessed is he who comes in the name of the Lord, even the King of Israel.'"
John 12:13 ESV

That was a marvelous day, wasn't it? The word that they shouted out that day was "Hosanna" which was recognition of the salvation that Jesus came to bring to them and to us. He is the King of kings and the Lord of lords. But in just five days these same people would exchange the word hosanna for crucify. They would deny that he was their King but rather they had no king but Caesar.

Upon first thought one might say that Jesus failed but the true triumph was that the reason he came was to die, it was to be crucified. So the people were correct in saying 'hosanna, save us Lord". They were correct because the King of kings duty was to die for them in order to save them.

Now, let me place another thought in your mind to think about. Did you know that when you repented of your sins and asked Jesus to be the King of your life and Lord of your ways, Jesus took up residency in you? This was His "Triumphant Entry" into your life as King of kings and Lord of lords, He has saved you. Hosannah! He came to bring salvation and when you believed Him to be God's only begotten Son celebration was heard in heaven. Blessed is He Who came in the name of the Lord!

There is another day of Triumphant that we read of in **Revelation 21:9 – 11** and that is of that New Jerusalem coming down out of heaven to earth where Jesus would be worshiped for eternity. That prepared New City of God! I like the words: I shall wipe away all tears; these are the words of He who is Faithful and True. It is He Who has made all things new! Old things have passed away and all that is there is spanking brand new. The Alpha and Omega, the Beginning and the End, the Lamb our Eternal King. We will shout: *"Hosanna! Blessed is he who comes in the name of the Lord, even the King of Israel."* **John 12:13 ESV**

Think about it. *Selah!*

Day 75:
Poured Out for Christ

"Even if I am to be poured out as a drink offering upon the sacrificial offering of your faith, I am glad and rejoice with you all. Likewise, you also should be glad and rejoice with me." **Philippians 2:17 & 18 ESV**

"Don't cry over spilt milk." I'm sure you have heard that idiom. If you spill a drink, it's gone and there is nothing that can be done. Therefore, just get on with life. Your choice is you can live happily after the event or you can live a disgruntled life. The choice is yours. Actually, this is a positive thing not a negative thing. Better things are ahead.

In our lives, we experience a lot of spills but Paul is talking about being poured out on purpose. This is not accidental but rather a plan, God's plan. These are times of pouring not accidental spills. In **Psalm 37:8** David discourages us from fretting over things because fretting will only make things worse. We fret over things that we feel helpless. So, my question is: What are you crying over?

The Apostle Paul here tells those believers in the church at Philippi that, if he is to be poured out on their behalf he desires that they understand that he chooses to be happy about it. He requests that his friends be happy as well and enter into this rejoicing with him.

A lot of believers have been poured out for Christ. Many believers have given their lives as martyrs for Christ and have gladly done so. More likely than not, we will see more and more believers will be called upon to be poured out for Christ. But don't cry over such a pouring it is for a purpose. Have the mind of Christ in you and the example of Paul to encourage you. To be used of Christ is our desire and how He chooses to use us is something to rejoice over not cry over. Nothing God does is useless or ineffective.

Have you ever heard the name **Polycarp**? He was born in 69 AD in Smyrna, (Izmir, Turkey) and died in Smyrna in 155 AD. Polycarp was the Bishop of the church in Smyrna and died a martyr. His life was poured out for Christ. The account of his death was taken from a letter that was sent to the churches of the area. The letter was from an eye-witness of his death. This letter is the earliest account of martyrdom outside the New Testament account of Stephen. **Acts 7**.

Polycarp was a disciple of John the Beloved. John Fox in his classic book: <u>Fox's Book of Martyrs</u> gives this account of the 86-year-old pastor:

Polycarp hearing that persons were seeking for him, escaped, but was discovered by a child. After feasting the guards who apprehended him, he desired an hour in prayer, which being allowed, he prayed with such fervency, that his guards repented that they had been instrumental in taking him. He was, however, carried before the proconsul, condemned, and burnt in the market place. The proconsul then urged him, saying, 'Swear, and I will release thee;-reproach Christ.'

Polycarp answered, 'Eighty and six years have I served Him, and He never once wronged me; how then shall I blaspheme my King, Who hath saved me?'"

As the fire was lit, the letter records, the flames refused to touch Polycarp, they seemed to arch around him. It was then that the proconsul had a soldier pierce him with a sword, which killed him. From his piercing, there came such a flood of blood that as it poured out it extinguished the fire.

When God calls you, He has a plan. Don't worry, don't fret and don't cry over the pouring, it is not a spill, it is not a loss it is a heavenly opportunity and time for refilling, refreshing and revival. When we know for certain of our eternal future there is cause for us to rejoice and be glad for great is your reward in heaven.

"Even if I am to be poured out as a drink offering upon the sacrificial offering of your faith, I am glad and rejoice with you all. Likewise, you also should be glad and rejoice with me." **Philippians 2:17 & 18 ESV**

Think about it. *Selah!*

Day 76:
What Is the Purpose?

"Now is my soul troubled. And what shall I say? Father, save me from this hour? But for this purpose I have come to this hour. 'Father, glorify your name' Then a voice came from heaven: 'I have glorified it, and I will glorify it again.'"
John 12:27 & 28 ESV

Are you troubled? Are you in the midst of a great struggle of life and wondering why is this happening to me; or why is this happening to someone else? Does life seem unfair?

Well, the truth is life does seem unfair and life certainly is filled with all types and various levels of uncertainty and confusion. We find ourselves in the grip of unforeseen trouble and difficulty. Why? Doesn't God see? Why does He not answer my prayer or the prayer of the faithful?

"What shall I say? Father, save me from this hour? But for this purpose I have come to this hour. Father, glorify your name." Did you get all that? Jesus was expressing confusion that He was experiencing at that moment and exampling how we should see it. It is not save me from this difficulty, this trouble or this tragedy but help me see how to view this. There is purpose in our life, God is not taken by surprise, we are taken by surprise. It is not God Who does not know what to do it is we on earth who are in doubt. What we need is to see the glory of the moment, the triumph that is about to take place.

God will reveal to us the fact that He has glorified us in the past and He is about to do the same for this moment. Trust Him in this moment for He is trustworthy. Though there is a full cup to suffer, He is with us as we drink that cup for Him and glory will be a result of this hour.

It is not the trouble in the moment that is most important, it is how we view the moment and the conclusion and the eternity that is a result of our obedience and struggle through this hour. Did you know that there is great joy in expressing: *"Father, glorify Your child."* Don't save me from this hour but be with me in this hour.

"Now is my soul troubled. And what shall I say? Father, save me from this hour? But for this purpose, I have come to this hour. 'Father, glorify your name' Then a voice came from heaven: 'I have glorified it, and I will glorify it again.'" **John 12:27 & 28 ESV**

Think about it. *Selah!*

Day 77:
Leave the Driving To Us

"Now is my soul troubled. And what shall I say? Father, save me from this hour? But for this purpose, I have come to this hour. 'Father, glorify your name.' Then a voice came from heaven: 'I have glorified it, and I will glorify it again.' "
John 12:27 & 28 ESV

Did you know that there are no accidents in the will of God? There are no slip-ups and no surprises. God will never say: *"Wow! I didn't see that coming!"*

There are, however, opportunities to be poured out for Christ. There are occasions in our lives where we can be especially used for Christ. It is in these awesome moments that God works in extraordinary ways and brings about extraordinary things and He provides us with all that is needed in those extraordinary opportunities.

These are moments where we may be poured out for Christs glory and honor. In such a moment Paul writes that he rejoices in it and he ask that the church rejoice with him in that moment. **Philippians 2:17 & 18**

Remember these things:

- God is never mistaken; He is never taken by surprise.
- Nothing ever troubles God and He asks us not to be troubled as well.

- There is never a moment in time, past, present or future, where God is unprepared.
- Though God may be challenged, He cannot be overcome.
- God never worries, doubts or ponders anything.
- There is never an occasion where He must scheme or plot to achieve His will. He uses all thing; good bad and ugly, together in the fashioning of good. And Though they may have been meant for evil purposes, He uses those very things for good and His glory.

What I am saying is this: Don't worry fellow believer in your journey through this life just relax, rejoice and rest in the Lord. Greyhound Bus Line used to have the slogan: *"Take Greyhound and leave the driving to us."* God says: *"Just get on the bus and leave all your trouble, worry and fuss."* It is a joy to be in God's Will, to be used for His purposes.

Humanly, Jesus was troubled but divinely He was committed and took glory in the purpose for which He came. We have moments where we are troubled and in those moments, turn your eyes on Christ and leave it all to Him.

"Now is my soul troubled. And what shall I say? Father, save me from this hour? But for this purpose I have come to this hour. 'Father, glorify your name.' Then a voice came from heaven: 'I have glorified it, and I will glorify it again.' "
John 12:27 & 28 ESV

Think about it. *Selah!*

Day 78:
What Is Good About Good Friday?

"and when he had given thanks he broke it, and said, 'This is my body which is for you. Do this in remembrance of me.'" **1 Corinthians 11:24 ESV**

Good Friday is the Friday before Easter. Friday is the day Jesus was crucified and put in the grave. Easter is the day, the day in which Jesus had been proclaiming that He would raise from the grave. By the way, Jesus said that "On the third day, not after the third day, that he would be raised from the grave. **Matthew 16:21** *"From that time Jesus began to show his disciples that he must go to Jerusalem and suffer many things from the elders and chief priests and scribes, and be killed, and on the third day be raised."* **ESV**   The religious leaders understood this fact as well as stated in **Matthew 27:64**.

Since sin entered into this world sacrifices have been made for the sin of people and nations. In **Hebrews 9:22** we see that without the shedding of blood there is no forgiveness of sin. Why blood? Because sin brought death into this world and the life is in the blood Scripture tells us. **Leviticus 17:11** *"For the life of the flesh is in the blood, and I have given it for you on the altar to make atonement for your souls, for it is the blood that makes atonement by the life."* **ESV**

All these sacrifices were ineffective in the forgiveness of sin. **Hebrews 10:4** Therefore, it was necessary for an effective, proper and acceptable sacrifice to be made and that sacrifice was the Lamb of God, Jesus Christ. He is called the Lamb because He was the worthy unspotted and unblemished sacrifice. *"But when Christ had offered for all time a single sacrifice for sins, he sat down at the right hand of God."* Now that is Good News! There is no other name given among men where by we can be saved. **Acts 4:12**

203

That sacrifice was the perfect sacrifice and a Good Sacrifice. It happened on Friday and therefore we call that Friday, GOOD FRIDAY! It is on this day that Christians come together to celebrate and remember that perfect sacrifice with the Lord's Table. Paul tells the believers in Corinth: *"For I received from the Lord what I delivered to you, that the Lord Jesus on the night when he was betrayed took bread, and when he had given thanks, he broke it, and said, 'This is my body which is for you. Do this in remembrance of me. In the same way, also he took the cup, after supper saying, 'This cup is the new covenant in by blood. Do this, as often as you drink it, in remembrance of me. For as often as you eat this bread and drink this cup, you proclaim the Lord's death until he comes."* **1 Corinthians 11:23 – 26 ESV**

So, as you celebrate **Good Friday** *"Remember this until he comes"*. The pain that Jesus endured was not good, the betrayal that He experienced was not good, the desertion of His friends was not good, nor was the grief that He suffered good. But the redemption that He secured was not only good but also lasting. That redemptive act was for me and it was for you! And that makes it GOOD! We receive it freely but it was not cheap, it required the blood of the Lamb of God; God's Only Begotten Son Jesus.

May I ask this question? Have you received His costly gift? If not, you can right now. Tell Jesus that you accept His sacrifice and repent of your sins. Tell Him that you realize that He is the only acceptable sacrifice and therefore the only way to eternal life in heaven. Tell Him that you not only take Him as Savior but as Lord of your life and soon coming King of Glory. Thank Him for that Gift and believe.

In **John 3:18** Jesus tells Nicodemus that unbelievers are condemned already because they have not believed that Jesus is the Son of God who is the only one who can take the sin of the world away. The reason Jesus came, my friend, is for you. And that is Good News!

"and when he had given thanks he broke it, and said, 'This is my body which is for you. Do this in remembrance of me.'" **1 Corinthians 11:24 ESV**

Think about it. *Selah!*

Day 79:
Are You a Grumbler?

"Therefore, my beloved brothers, be steadfast, immovable, always abounding in the Lord, knowing that in the Lord your labor is not in vain."
1 Corinthians 15:58 ESV

Are you a grumbler? I ask myself this question and as I begin to review how I live my life I must regretfully say, yes, I believe that I am. I call myself an optimist and one would think that an optimist should be an encourager. But as I think about myself I begin to see many moments I spent thinking about situations and events that I find opportunity to complain.

The children of Israel often found themselves murmuring to Moses and God about discomforts. The murmurings were evidence of too much time spent in thinking and sharing with others the discontent of their situation. They were at the brink of revolt. They had the evidence in hand and they felt justified in bringing the complaint to Moses. To the people, the complaint was valid and reasonable. I'm sure Moses at times felt like giving up and leaving these people.

That is how I feel with my meditated complaints, grumbling and murmuring brought before God in prayer; at times, I feel good about it. How about you, have you ever experienced such feelings? Have you ever prayed about something that was a nuisance in your life or inconvenience in your life? It could be that we label that complaint as "spiritual", "Scriptural" or a "Godly" complaint. Does your discontent make you think of previous places in your life were you wonder why in the world did you leave in the first place? Are you yearning for past places of experienced blessings?

Perhaps your complaint has to do with those around you are just too "ungodly" and you want God to remove you from it. It could be in your job, your church, or your neighborhood that you want to be removed. Now your complaint could be valid but may I ask that you consider one other element in your complaint: What do you feel was the purpose that God placed you there in the first place? Have you fulfilled the purpose or have you brought to completion that goal and God's purpose for sending your there? It could be that you have finished your work, completed that purpose of God but the question still remains. Ask yourself this question: Is it actually God Who is leading you away or the problems? That question must still be contemplated. Are you giving up or have you completed the work?

Now, there are times when we must *"shake off the dust from our shoes"* but still we must make sure it is God Who is leading us and not we ourselves or another person. That is a difficult decision but we must not make them quickly or without thought. It is in these situations that we must make sure we have spent time before the Holy Spirit allowing Him to direct, to correct and to bring peace to our lives.

Now I don't want to be known as a grumbler, I want to be known by others as one who is faithful, steadfast and unmovable in the things of God but also to be known as a listener, an encourager and source of knowledge, understanding and wisdom to others. I want to stand before God as a faithful servant not a grumbling one. I want to be remembered as a dependable friend and acquaintance. I want others to see Jesus in me. Jesus, stood and looked out at Jerusalem and wept. He stayed with those ungodly, hateful, perverse and self-righteous people and remained with them until He had finished the work that the Father had sent Him to do. As He was raised and fixed with nails to the cross, His response was: "Father forgive them for they know not what they do." Jesus is our example.

So, here is the question: Am I grumbling? What you are discontented with may be a legitimate error that needs to be corrected but is it a reason for you to leave? This is not an easy question to answer but is your labor actually in vain?

"Therefore, my beloved brothers, be steadfast, immovable, always abounding in the Lord, knowing that in the Lord your labor is not in vain."
1 Corinthians 15:58 ESV

Think about it. *Selah!*

210

Day 80:
Can A Dead Person Live?

"Now if Christ is proclaimed as raised from the dead, how can some of you say that there is not resurrection of the dead? But if there is not resurrection from the dead, then not even Christ has been raised." **1 Corinthians 15:12 & 13 ESV**

Can a dead man live? We might say no, a dead man is dead and cannot be brought back to life. History itself tells us that there have been occasions where a person was dead or at least thought to be dead and restored to life. Jesus raised Lazarus from the dead. Elijah and Elisha are noted as bring to life those who were dead. There are many doctors, missionaries, evangelists and others who have reportedly witnessed those who have been declared dead and life was somehow brought back to them.

But when we read in Scripture of resurrection, what is meant is resurrection from the dead to "Eternal Life". **Hebrews 9:27** *"And just as it is appointed for man to die once, and after that comes judgment."* **ESV Romans 6:23** tells us: *"For the wages of sin is death, but the free gift of God is eternal life in Christ Jesus our Lord."* **ESV**

The answer to "Can a dead person live again?" is yes. Just as Jesus was raised from the grave, so too the believer will be raised from death to eternal life in Christ Jesus our Lord. Lazarus and all the others who were brought back from death eventually died or will die. Here is the truth. Every person will die once but they do not have to die twice. There are two parts to a person; one is physical and the other is spiritual. To live upon this earth takes a physical birth. To live in heaven with God, Who is a spirit takes a spiritual birth. We call that being born again. If you are born twice, physically and spiritually, it results in eternal life. If you are born once and never bring life to your spiritual body, you will die twice. You will die on earth and eternal death in hell with Satan and his angels. *"Blessed and holy is the one who shares in the first resurrection! Over such the second death has no power, but they will be priest of God and of Christ, and they will reign with him for a thousand years."* **Revelation 20:6 ESV** "For as by the one man's disobedience the many were made sinners, so by one man's obedience the many will be made righteous." **Romans 5:18 ESV**

The correct question is: Can a person who dies on this earth live forever? Yes, a person can if they have been born again. We can also say is it possible for a dead person to die again? And the answer is yes, if they have not been born again.

What about you? Have you been born again? Are you sure that you have been born again. The evidence of a living person is that they do thinks a living person does naturally. Does your earthly life reflect the things of a spiritual life? Just asking.

Eternal life comes by take the eternal life of Christ. Eternal life is a free gift and it is received by our believing in, trusting in and relying upon the living Christ. Jesus asks of us that we repent of our dead and sinful life and accepting the living and pure righteousness of Jesus upon our life. If your life has not been reflective of the living

Christ draw near God and He will draw near you. Resist the devil and he will flee. **James 4: 7 & 8**

Can a dead person live again? Yes. If we are in Christ Jesus we are new creations and the old is passed away and behold all things are made new. New body, new life all things are new. **Ephesians 2:5 & 6; Revelation 21:5**

"Now if Christ is proclaimed as raised from the dead, how can some of you say that there is not resurrection of the dead? But if there is not resurrection from the dead, then not even Christ has been raised." **1 Corinthians 15:12 & 13 ESV**

Think about it. *Selah!*

Day 81:
Because Of Christ

"But by the grace of God I am what I am, and his grace toward me was not in vain. On the contrary, I work harder than any of them, though it was not I, but the grace of God that is with me." **1 Corinthians 15:10 ESV**

God's grace is sufficient for all things but that doesn't mean that there will not be times of difficulty. I frequently recite: **John 16:23 ESV** *"In the world you will have tribulation."* (this is suffering and opposition). Jesus tells us that we are to expect trouble because the world is trouble. Jesus follows this with a statement of His grace: *"but take heart, I have overcome the world."* (Grace).

The work of the world is trouble, suffering, disease, opposition and the like. The work of Christ has produced mercy, grace and love for the believer. These are in the make up of our faith and our faith is our shield in time of trouble. *"In all circumstances take up the shield of faith."* **Ephesians 6:16 ESV** What is our faith? Our faith is in the work of Jesus Christ for us. We overcome and win because of Christ and His own work. We don't overcome our fight. Jesus has fought for us and has already won the victory, He has already overcome the foe.

I love the verse in **2 Chronicles 20:17** *"You will not need to fight in this battle. Stand firm, hold your position, and see that salvation of the Lord on your behalf, O Judah and Jerusalem. Do not be afraid and do not be dismayed.*

Tomorrow go out against them and the Lord will be with you." **ESV**   No, we do not need to fight this battle for the Lord has won. What is needed on our behalf is to *"Stand firm, hold your position,"*

Has the world captured your attention by opposition? Do you find your mind going to places that it need not be? Do you find it difficult to stay your mind upon Christ? Then, here is what you must do, what you must do is to focus on Christ, stand firm in His strength and hold your position. You do not need to fight here because in this battle, it is God who will do the fighting for you. Do you understand that God is with you? The battle is where God is working for you and He does it because of what His Son, Jesus Christ has done for you and promised you.

Holding one's position requires work. Now, God gives grace for the battle but we still must work hard and stand firm.   Standing firm requires diligence, it requires determination, and it requires energy. We stand firm and we stand committed to that which God has called us to do. So, don't give up, don't give in, stand in your faith, it is God who is at work and He is in you.

"But by the grace of God I am what I am, and his grace toward me was not in vain. On the contrary, I work harder than any of them, though it was not I, but the grace of God that is with me." **1 Corinthians 15:10 ESV**

Think about it. *Selah!*

Day 82:
Casting Aside

"Humble yourselves, therefore, under the mighty hand of God so that at the proper time he may exalt you, casting all your anxieties on him, because he cares for you." **1 Peter 5:6 & 7 ESV**

Have you ever found yourself in the grip of someone or something that shows no mercy or grace toward you? Have you ever been under an attack where there seems to be no one to help? Have you ever been in a situation where you are totally helpless as is all others around you? Have you ever felt as though no one really cares for you or has any concern whatsoever?

That type of situation brings about great anxiety to you, doesn't it? What do you do at times like that? You worry and begin to think: "Doesn't anyone care? No, you think, no one really cares for me at all."

It is in these type of situations, that God proves Himself to be a very present help. He is not a future hope or a past hope; He is a "very present" hope. You see, God never leaves you and He never forsakes you. God is personally with us right now. In **1 Peter 5:7** we are encouraged to cast all our fears and anxieties upon Him or to cast aside all our fears and anxieties because He cares for us. Does anyone care? Yes, someone cares; God cares. And if God cares for us then why should anyone or anything else matter anyway? If God is for us who could be against us? **Romans 8:31**

Notice what Peter says here: *"Humble yourselves, therefore, under the mighty hand of God so that at the proper time he may exalt you."* You are God's child and He will bring relief "at the proper time". Martha and Mary both expressed anxiety when they said: *"If you had been here my brother would not have died."* **John 11:21 & 32** They were right, if Jesus would have been there when they called for Him, Lazarus would not have died. But notice what the response of Jesus to the reprimand of his disciples in **verse 40**: *"that if you believe you will see the glory of God."* This was the right time. This was God's timing. God works His will in your life for His glory and for your faith.

I love Tommy Walkers song: <u>I Cast My Eyes On You</u>. He writes in the first verse:

"I fix my eyes on You, the Author of my faith,
casting aside every sin and every weight.
I fix my eyes on you, I lay my burdens down,
Letting the cares of this world now fade away."
Tommy Walker

Sins and weights should be cast aside in the forgiveness the Blood of Jesus cleanses. Burdens and cares of this world need to be cast aside and placed on Him and when that is done, they fade away. The first actions by us is to "fix our eyes on Jesus Christ".

Here is the question: Are you burdened today? Do you feel helpless because the cares of this world have overtaken you? Are there sins and weights in your life that are holding you down? Do you feel that no one really cares about you? Well, there is someone who cares about you and He died for you. That person is Jesus Christ, He cares for you so humble yourself before Him, cast all your cares upon Him, because He really does care for you. Now be patient and at the right time, His mighty hand will come down on those cares and anxieties.

"Humble yourselves, therefore, under the mighty hand of God so that at the proper time he may exalt you, casting all your anxieties on him, because he cares for you." **1 Peter 5:6 & 7 ESV**

Think about it. *Selah!*

Day 83:
Only A Week End Job

"He is not here, but is risen. Remember how he told you, while he was still in Galilee, that the Son of man must be delivered into the hands of sinful men and be crucified and on the third day rise." **Luke 24:6 & 7**

Have you ever wondered if you were beyond help? Have you ever thought: "I would like to become a Christian but there are just too many things in my life that I need to get fixed? Have you ever wondered if Jesus would even want to forgive the sins of your life because they are too great or terrible?

Have you ever thought about this: Did you know that the combined efforts of Satan and his angels battling against God's creation, bringing sin upon man and trying to over throw God's plan; (and he has a lot of angels the Bible says that when he was cast out of heaven he took with him one third of all the created angels of heaven. **Revelation 12:4 & 9**); all their battle against God combined, which covers 4,000 years and more before the coming of Christ; and all the sin heaped up through the next 2,000 years after Jesus ascended to heaven and continuing on through the last sin committed on the last day of time; Jesus made atonement for in one week end? Jesus conquered death, sin and the grave with His righteous blood sacrifice and resurrection all in one week ends work of redemption.

His sacrifice was so great that after He had made it He sat down, work done, God's wrath satisfied . . . finished in one week end. His blood was poured out for us and all sins atoned for, blotted out forever! Your sin is but a few among them all.

There is only one condition. There is only one missing factor and that condition, that missing factor is that His gift, His sacrifice, His redeeming work must be received. Have you received it? **John 3:18** tells us that Jesus did not come to condemn anyone but rather to save the world. That salvation work includes you. That work happened in one Holy Week End that we call Easter, where we celebrate His Resurrection.

So, where do you stand? The cure is offered for your sin, the forgiveness is certain but have you received Jesus Christ as your Savior and Lord? You receive His gift by saying: Lord Jesus, I believe that You are the Only Begotten Son of God Who was sent to his world to pay the price for Sin. I believe that You are that Sacrifice and I repent of my sinful life. I accept your gift of Eternal Life. I want you to be Lord of my life. Take my sin, and cleanse me with your righteousness and make me a new creation. I thank You Lord, I believe You Lord and I will live for You all the days of my life.

If you did that you are a new creation of Christ Jesus and a member of the heavenly family of God. Jesus will be coming for you to take you to the place that He is preparing for you.

All sin is bad. There is no sin that is not so bad. Sin keeps us from heaven but Jesus makes us fit for heaven and worthy to stand before a holy God. What He did on that Easter weekend was for you!

"He is not here, but is risen. Remember how he told you, while he was still in Galilee, that the Son of man must be delivered into the hands of sinful men and be crucified and on the third day rise." **Luke 24:6 & 7 ESV**

Think about it. *Selah!*

Day 84:
Playing A Part, Your Part

*"But as it is, God arranged the members in the body, each one of them as he chose. If all were a single member, where would the body be? As it is, there are many parts, yet one body."***1 Corinthians 12:19 & 20 ESV**

The world-renowned neurosurgeon and 2016 Presidential candidate, Dr. Ben Carson has noted: *"Regardless of ones position in life we can all play a part in the next generations life."*

Did you know that you play an important role in the life of others? Do your realize that God has given you a special talent and ability that no one else is able to provide in the way that you do? Have you ever thought about the fact that it is God Who has entrusted you with that talent and ability to make a positive difference in the life of someone? You may not realize it but the one who questions your role and importance in the life of others is not outer that Satan and his angles. Any thought of insignificance that you may have did not come from God but from Satan. So, make a choice in your life, come to a good understanding with yourself; who will you choose to listen? Will it be God or will it be the forces of evil?

You play an important role! The Apostle Paul writes to the believers in the church at Corinth: *"But as it is, God arranged the members in the body, each one of them as he chose"* **1 Corinthians 12:19 ESV** You are where you are and possess the ability that you have by the hand of God. As the body has many members so also does the church, he goes on to say. You do not need to have the abilities of someone else, that would be redundant. The person that you have your mind on does not have the special abilities that you do and even if the did they would not be able to do what you do or make the impact that you can.

So, Thank God for what He has done through you. There are others who are thanking God for you and you don't even know it. But you will come to that understanding at the Judgment Seat of Christ. **Romans 14:12; 2 Corinthians 5:10; & Hebrews 4:13**

I know that we all experience the fact of joyfully accepting our mission in life at times: *"I believe; help my unbelief."* **Mark 9:24 ESV** Here is my word of encouragement: Play your part and play it well. The little triangle has it role in the concerto of life.

"But as it is, God arranged the members in the body, each one of them as he chose. If all were a single member, where would the body be? As it is, there are many parts, yet one body." **1 Corinthians 12:19 & 20 ESV**

Think about it. *Selah!*

Day 85:
I Believe Help My Unbelief.

"Immediately the father of the child cried out and said, 'I believe, help my unbelief!" **Mark 9:24 ESV**

On January 27, 2015, a Poignant commemoration took place at Auschwitz; the infamous concentrations camp in Poland. It was the 70ᵗʰ anniversary of the liberation of the camp by the Russian Army on January 27, of 1945. Reporters Matthew Day and Joe Shute, of the British newspaper: "The Telegraph" covered the event and documented the comments of Arek Hersh, a Holocaust survivor with the number B7608 tattooed on his arm.

Arek informed them that he was taken there in 1944 and was subsequently liberated by the Russian Army on January 27, 1945, made the comment: *"It was –9 degrees Fahrenheit when I was liberated. I had only my pajama uniform on. I shudder every time I think about this place. I can't control the fear. Every time I come here I feel fearful. I was 14 and counted among the 185 children who came. Only two of the children survived and I was one of the two. When I think of all the terrible things that happened to us: how we lived, how we died. It's a reminder of what men can do to each other."*

When they were liberated I am sure it was hard for them to believe and for days, months and even years there was still the lingering fear the captivated their minds. Though 70 years after the liberation, still Mr. Hersh found it hard to believe what happened those final two years as a captive. He could say as the father in **Mark 9:24**: *"I believe, help my unbelief!"* **ESV**

Found carved into the wall of an Auschwitz barrack were these, now famous lyrics:

"I believe in the sun,
Even when it is not shining.
I believe in love,
Even when I cannot feel it.
I believe in God,
Even when He is silent."
Unknown

To believe in something does not always mean that we never doubt or fear. But to truly believe in something is be fearless and confident. Fear can captivate ones whole being. Jesus commented to the believing yet still unbelieving father, *"If you can! All things are possible for one who believe."* **Verse 23 ESV** Jesus was saying to the father of the boy: What do you mean: "IF" you can! Don't you believe that I can? You do understand that the only hindrance here is unbelief. So, do you believe? And then comes the father's answer which tells the whole story: Yes Lord, I do believe but I need help with my weakness of belief.

Isn't that often true in your life? I can tell you that sadly it is often true in my life as well. I worry about things that I know God can do and is in the process of doing but with all my understanding, belief and trust in God, I still find myself helplessly drowning in my fear of unbelief. As Arek Hersh admitted: *"I shudder every time I think about this place. I can't control the fear. Every time I come here I feel fearful."* He had been liberated for 70 years, yet still the fear often overtook him.

Still today I find myself crying out to God: Yes, God I believe you and trust you yet, I still find myself in the needless grip of unbelief. Help my unbelief. Our help comes from the Lord; Who is a very present help in time of our trouble. He is our Rock, our Fortress our Strong Tower. He is here with me and will never leave me. He is greater than anything that may come against me. He loves me. He is faithful to me. He will never leave me. He hears my prayer and knows my need before I even ask, He has never failed me in the past. He tells me that I should expect trouble, in this world of trouble but to be of good cheer because He has already overcome the world. He cannot lie. He hand is upon me, and I believe all these things. Lord, would you help me in my unbelief.

Have you noticed here that Jesus healed the boy? Yes, Jesus did help the father's unbelief and He also helps us in our moments of unbelief. When moments of unbelief come into your life, ask for help. Jesus knows our heart, He knows our weakness and in our weakness, He will make us strong and whole again. Lift up your head! Your redemptions is soon coming.

"Immediately the father of the child cried out and said, 'I believe, help my unbelief!" **Mark 9:24 ESV**

Think about it. *Selah!*

Day 86:
What Is It That Hardens
A Believers Heart?

"Why are you discussing the fact that you have no bread? Do you not yet perceive or understand? Are your hearts hardened?" **Mark 8:17 ESV**

Hardened arteries is a disorder in which arteries (blood vessels that carry oxygenated blood from the heart to other parts of the body) become narrowed by deposited fat which will block the flow of blood to the heart and will soon prompt a heart attack or stroke.

Hardened arteries are caused by a buildup of fat (cholesterol deposits called atherosclerosis) first deposited on the inside wall of the arteries which then become hardened by fibrous tissue and calcification or plaque and is the cause of heart attacks and strokes. High blood pressure, a sedentary lifestyle, and obesity are all major risk factors for atherosclerosis.

I have had a heart attack as well as a stroke. I thank the Lord that the heart attack as well as the stroke was very mild and not debilitating. May I make a comparison here? When the life style of a believer in Christ Jesus takes up a sedentary lifestyle, and contented with the richness of Gods blessing in his life, he is then in danger of a hardening of the heart. When we become inactive in our mission in life and seek more and more blessing then we are in danger of a hardened heart.

The disciples of Jesus were discussing and apparently worried about the amount of bread they had. Only one loaf! How as that to feed 12 disciples? The could not see, they could not hear nor could they remember, Jesus rebuked. **Vs. 18** *"Do you not yet understand?'* **vs. 21 ESV**

The truth here is that Jesus is one only sufficient but more than sufficient to meet our needs. If we believe that then, why would we worry? Why would we waste our time discussing things that are already taken care of?

Do you find yourself worrying, discussing with yourself and others about things that seem not to be going as you feel they should? I am guilty of this for sure. What has happened is we have allowed the life-giving flow of God's provision to be blocked by the fatty buildup of worldly fat in our lives. We are idlily eating the richness of the food from God's table, and forgotten His hand in our lives.

So, ponder a while on the provision of God in your life. Look around you and see what God is doing in the lives of others and rejoice in it with them. Listen to the joy of fellow believers telling of God's hand in their lives. Remember these things and give God the glory for them and the life giving flow of the Holy Spirit in our lives will spark activity and cut down on the buildup of worry in our lives.

"Why are you discussing the fact that you have no bread? Do you not yet perceive or understand? Are your hearts hardened?" **Mark 8:17 ESV**
Think about it. *Selah!*

Day 87:
Veritas

"Then Pilate said to him, 'So your are a king?' Jesus answered, 'You say that I am a king. For this purpose I was born and for this purpose I have come into the world to bear witness of the truth. Everyone who is of the truth listens to my voice. Pilate said to him, 'what is truth?'" **John 18:37 & 38 ESV**

Veritas is Latin for truth. Many schools, colleges and universities have for its motto the word veritas. The search for truth has been the quest of many throughout the ages and men still seek truth today. The problem in our search for truth is having some idea as to what real truth is. Truth can only be found with an honest search.

Today, the intelligencia of this world rejects Scripture and Jesus, very source of truth, as truth and thus there is nothing but argument and disagreement. Jesus tells us that He is The Truth but His claim is disregarded. So the search goes on and it will never be found. In the words of Pilate: *"What is truth?"* **vs. 38**

What about you? Are you in a search for truth? Do you find yourself frequently confused about life? When you find truth, you must trust truth and when things come against what you know is truth, you must disregard it as "non-truth" or a lie. *Remember there is no confusion with truth, for truth is fact and it can be trusted even when all stands against it.* When truth is contested, All men are liars **Romans 3:3** *". . .Let God be true though every one were a liar,. . ."* and God is true and He is Truth.

Here is the principle: If you desire to find truth, real truth and nothing but the truth seek God and His righteous, pure and total truth. If you sincerely seek it you will definitely find it. As Pilate asked: *"What is truth?"* The Truth stood before Him. The Truth stands before you as well. Seek Him and you will find Him. As the Wise Men sought the Baby Jesus and found Him, so too do all those who diligently seek Him. They will find Him and in finding Him they find Truth.

Veritas, Truth, God's Word is Truth.

"Then Pilate said to him, 'So your are a king?' Jesus answered, 'You say that I am a king. For this purpose I was born and for this purpose I have come into the world to bear witness of the truth. Everyone who is of the truth listens to my voice. Pilate said to him, 'what is truth?'" **John 18:37 & 38 ESV**

Think about it. *Selah!*

Day 88:
Ephphatha

And looking up to heaven, he sighed and said to him, 'Ephphatha' that is, be opened.' And his ears were opened, his tongue was released, and he spoke plainly."
Mark 7:34 & 35 ESV

I have a hearing problem. It is embarrassing not to be able to hear clearly and distinctly. Having to frequently say: "What did you say?" or to ask of another person: "What did he or she say?" I definitely need a hearing aid but I jokingly tell people; it is cheaper to say "What" than to buy a hearing aid.

In the book of **Mark** we read where Jesus meets a man who was not only deaf but who had a speech impediment as well. This man had a lot of good friends because they took him to Jesus and they "begged" Jesus to lay His hand upon the man and heal him. Jesus in turn took the deaf man aside to a private place and did some very unusual things:

1. He put his fingers into the deaf mans ears.
2. He spit and placed his finger upon the mans tongue
3. He looked up to heaven and said: *"Ephphatha"* (F – fa – tha).

At that point, the man's, Mark says, tongue was "released" and he spoke plainly. What an amazing moment that was. In **verse 37** of **chapter 7 Mark** writes of the response of the crowd: *"He has done all things well."*

Now, what do I want you to see here? Often we read in God's Word or hear God's Word proclaimed and we turn a *"deaf ear"* to it. Not only do we turn a deaf ear but we have difficulty understanding and articulating what God is saying to us. Jesus says to us: *"Ephphata,"* be opened. Are you open to the Word of God? His word to you is clear but what is it that is preventing the healing words of God from entering your ear? What is it that stands in the way of God's love to you? Remember He does all things well. All that God does for you is for your good. Remember, God has your eternal future in mind. Are you open to His word?

God's Word is for those who would hear it. But, do you want to hear what God is clearly saying to you?

Then there is one more thing that I would have you to pray. Pray for those missionaries all over the world who stand proclaiming God's Word to the lost and dying. Pray *"Ephphata",* be opened! May their ears be opened and receptive to the soul healing power of God's Word, of His Love, of His mercy and of His grace.

And looking up to heaven, he sighed and said to him, 'Ephphatha' that is, be opened.' And his ears were opened, his tongue was released, and he spoke plainly." **Mark 7:34 & 35 ESV**

Think about it. *Selah!*

Day 89:
Continue In What You Have Learned

"But as for you, continue in what you have learned and have firmly believed, knowing from whom you learned it and how from childhood you have been acquainted with the sacred writings which are able to make you wise from salvation through faith in Christ Jesus." **2 Timothy 3:14 & 15 ESV**

Here are a few things simply put that all believers must have a clear understanding and be able to relate to others, they are things we should know:

Glory: It is for God's alone
Faith: It comes from God alone to us to give us a way to approach God.
Trust or Belief: Our commitment to God.
Grace: God's tool to forgive us.
Mercy: God's tool for holding back punishment from us.
Forgiveness: Can only come from God and cannot be questioned.
Sovereign: God's right to do whatever He wishes and He cannot be questioned.
Atonement: The single transaction made on behalf of the believer, qualifies the believer for heaven and satisfies God to justly forgive our sin.
Reconciliation: God's work in securing for us a legal position and right before Him.
Baptism: Is our public statement or advertisement to others that we have been made a New Creation.

Righteousness: What Jesus alone possesses but shares it by covering the believer with it.

Blessings: God's gift to us.

Happiness and Joy: A choice or attitude in serving God.

Tithes: It is 10% of our finances. It belongs to God but He challenges us to cheerfully return to Him so we can experience His added blessing in live. God challenges us to try Him by our giving.

Offerings: Gifts to God and for His work. They reflect our heart.

Sacrifice: Doing without.

Suffering: Our duty and joy as a believer.

Prayer: Talking with God.

Scripture: God's Word, Him talking to us.

Church: The body of believers who come together to encourage and unite in worship and ministry.

Jesus: God's Only begotten Son

Holy Spirit: The Comforter, Teacher, Guide and Helper that Jesus left for us and
Who proceeds from the Father.

The Father: The first person of the Trinity, Jehovah, The Great I Am.

Trinity: The three-in-one

Gospel: The Good News that we have been entrusted with to take to people everywhere.

Learn them, and have them firmly etched in your mind and be able to relate to others in a simple way. They are part of every believer.

"But as for you, continue in what you have learned and have firmly believed, knowing from whom you learned it

and how from childhood you have been acquainted with the sacred writings which are able to make you wise from salvation through faith in Christ Jesus." **2 Timothy 3:14 & 15 ESV**

Think about it. *Selah!*

Day 90:
Can You Trust God?

"Blessed is the man who trusts in the Lord, whose trust is the Lord."
Jeremiah 17:7 ESV

How much can you trust God?

Do you trust Him completely?

Is there a limit to the trust that you have in God?

Yes! You might proclaim loudly. I trust Him completely and with my whole being all of the time! May be your reaction.

I feel certain that all believers would have the same response. But may I ask you to take a closer look. May I ask you to see if there are actual things in your life that may be holding you back as a believer from greater blessing, greater ministry and greater service to God.

If I were to continue with my questioning I would say:

- Can you trust God at His word? If He says something do you completely believe it? Do your actions reflect your answer?

- He said He who believes in me will have eternal life. Do you believe that?
- He said if you ask anything "according to my will" I will supply it. Do you believe that?
- He said He is coming back for us. Do you believe that?
- He said bring your tithe to storehouse and if we have any doubt about it to test Him at His word to see if He will not flood you with blessings in excess of what you need and rebuke the devourer as a proof of His Word. Do you believe that?

"Trust in the Lord with all your heart, and do not lean to your own understanding." **Proverbs 3:5 ESV** God's word proves true and will not return to Him empty. **Psalm 18:30 ESV Isaiah 55:11 ESV**

If God says it, it is true and you can trust in it. *"The grass withers, the flower fades, but the word of our God will stand forever."* **Isaiah 40:8 ESV**

"Bring the full tithe into the storehouse, that there may be food in my house. And there by put me to the test, says the Lord of hosts, if I will not open the windows of heaven for you and pour down for you a blessing until there is no more need." **Malachi 3:10 ESV**

Think about it. *Selah*

www.ingramcontent.com/pod-product-compliance
Lightning Source LLC
Chambersburg PA
CBHW071956040426
42447CB00009B/1354